IMAGES
of America

WATKINSVILLE FROM THE COLLECTION OF BOBBY GORDON

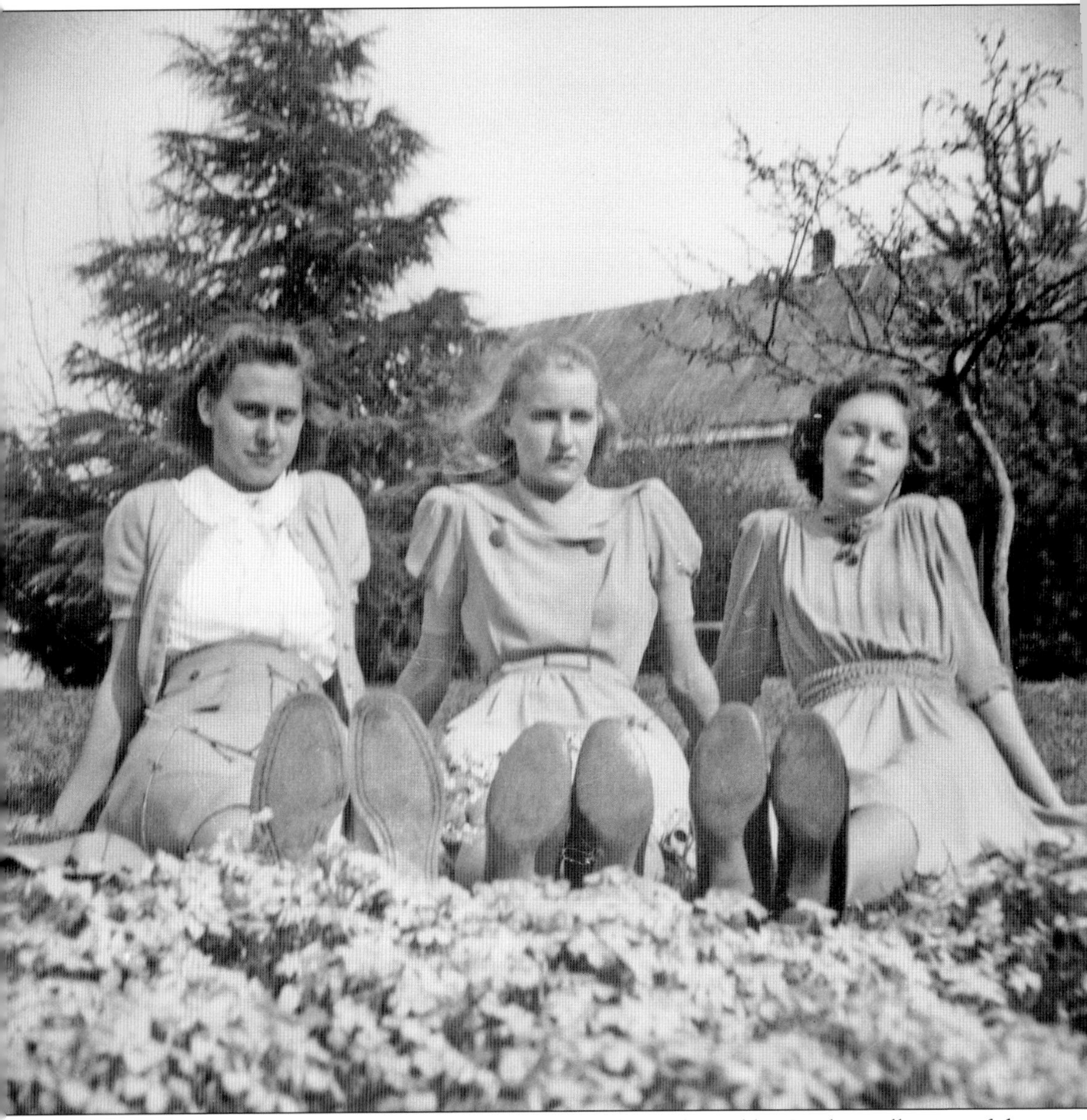

On the Cover: Based on the number of photographs in the Bobby Gordon collection of these three friends of Bobby's wearing the same dresses, one suspects he used a roll of film and posed them in different places around town. The girls above are, from left to right, Joan Camp, Anita Chandler, and Mary Ashford. On the cover, they are, from left to right, Anita Chandler, Joan Camp, and Mary Ashford. (Courtesy of the Bobby Gordon collection at the Oconee County Historical Society.)

IMAGES
of America

WATKINSVILLE FROM THE COLLECTION OF BOBBY GORDON

Hugh C. Gordon and Margaret F. Sommer
on behalf of the Oconee County Historical Society

ARCADIA
PUBLISHING

ISBN 978-1-4671-2922-0

Published by Arcadia Publishing
Charleston, South Carolina

Printed in the United States of America

Library of Congress Control Number: 2018958880

For all general information, please contact Arcadia Publishing:
Telephone 843-853-2070
Fax 843-853-0044
E-mail sales@arcadiapublishing.com
For customer service and orders:
Toll-Free 1-888-313-2665

Visit us on the Internet at www.arcadiapublishing.com

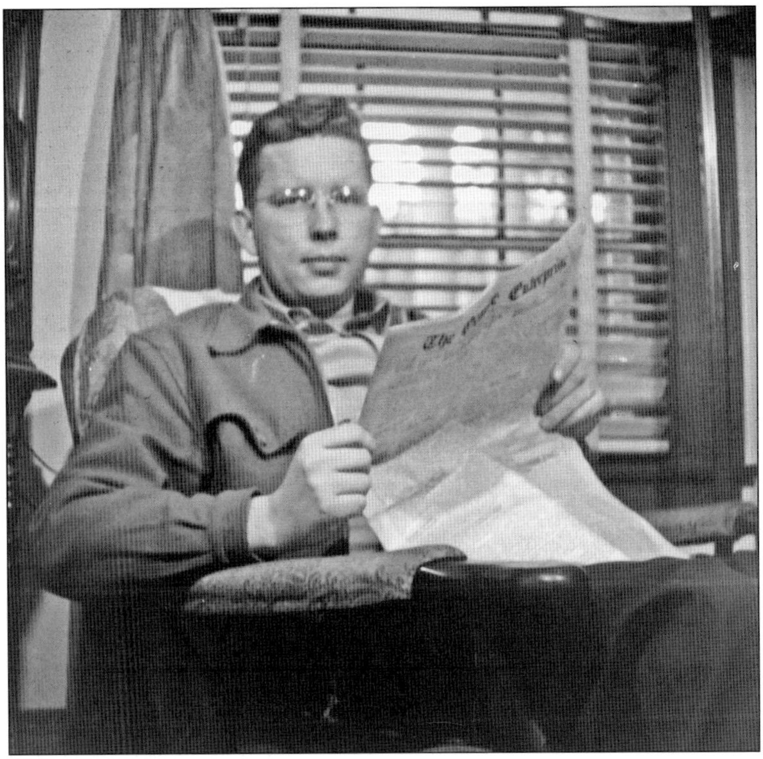

Robert Sydney Gordon, the photographer of the images in this book, reads the *Oconee Enterprise*, which has been the county's newspaper since 1884. (Courtesy of the Bobby Gordon collection at the Oconee County Historical Society.)

Contents

ACKNOWLEDGMENTS

The authors would like to thank the following people who helped us to identify those in the photographs, answered questions, and shared bits of information about the people and places in the book. Dr. Roy Ward, in a series of articles in the *Oconee Enterprise* in 1992 and in a photo book entitled *Pretty Close to Home*, provided information about many of the people in Bobby's photographs. Albert Ward and Larry Weatherford met with the authors to help identify people and to share some of their memories. Albert has also written several articles and photo books that were useful sources of information. Sarah Bell helped with proofreading and editing. Frank Houde provided information about the airplanes in the first chapter. The authors would also like to thank the Oconee County Historical Society for giving us permission to work on this project.

All images are from the Bobby Gordon collection at the Oconee County Historical Society.

Introduction

Robert "Bobby" Sydney Gordon was born on August 19, 1923, in Oconee County, Georgia. He was the third of four children of Hugh Bingham Gordon and Mary Osborne. He grew up and attended school in Watkinsville. He was a member of the Oconee High School class of 1940 and graduated from the University of Georgia with a degree in business administration in 1943.

As a teen, he became interested in photography and obtained a used camera with which he photographed high school friends, relatives, and townspeople in and around Watkinsville. This was a time when cameras were rare possessions, so everyone in town was willing to pose for him.

Bobby served in the Army during World War II as a radio operator with the 106th Cavalry. He had a camera with him during this period and took many photographs of fellow soldiers, towns, and vistas of Austria.

After the war, he returned home and became a charter member of the local Veterans of Foreign Wars and a member of the local American Legion post. He found a job with the agricultural extension service but continued to pursue his dream of becoming a videographer. He died suddenly of a brain aneurism on August 15, 1951, and was buried in the Watkinsville Cemetery on his 29th birthday. The *Oconee Enterprise* commented on August 24 that he "had many friends in Athens and elsewhere. He was loved by everyone. The entire community was saddened by his death."

In the years since, his photographs have periodically appeared in books by Albert and Dr. Roy Ward and in news articles. However, the entire collection has never been shared. Dr. Roy Ward was a well-known local physician, artist, and fellow photographer. He described a photography expedition with Bobby. They had a good time photographing the same things and then comparing the results. Dr. Roy Ward described Bobby as a "very friendly, sociable person." He thought Bobby's work was "unsophisticated and charming" and that it had the ability to "evoke for us now, the place and time better than any words." The photographs also show that Bobby had a sense of humor and was willing to experiment with his camera.

The passage of time makes it difficult to identify all the people and places he photographed. It also makes it impossible to give exact dates for each photograph. However, those willing to peruse this book will acquire an idea of what life was like in a small Georgia community during the 1930s and 1940s. The collection also shows that the topics that Bobby chose to photograph have not changed much from what people today photograph. Bobby took photographs of people around town, children, babies, and animals. He showed up at sporting events, accidents, and fires. He took advantage of new ways to look at the world. For example, he took his camera up in an airplane and hurried outside to take pictures during a rare Georgia snowstorm.

On October 21, 2002, a group of interested Oconee County citizens gathered at the William Daniel House to discuss whether to organize a historical society. By the end of 2003, the Oconee County Historical Society was incorporated. One concern of the society over the years has been collecting oral histories and scanning photographs and documents connected with Oconee County's history. Bobby's nephew Hugh Gordon, who has worked to digitalize Bobby's photographs, shared his work with the society and has given us permission to share them with the readers of this book.

One

WATKINSVILLE

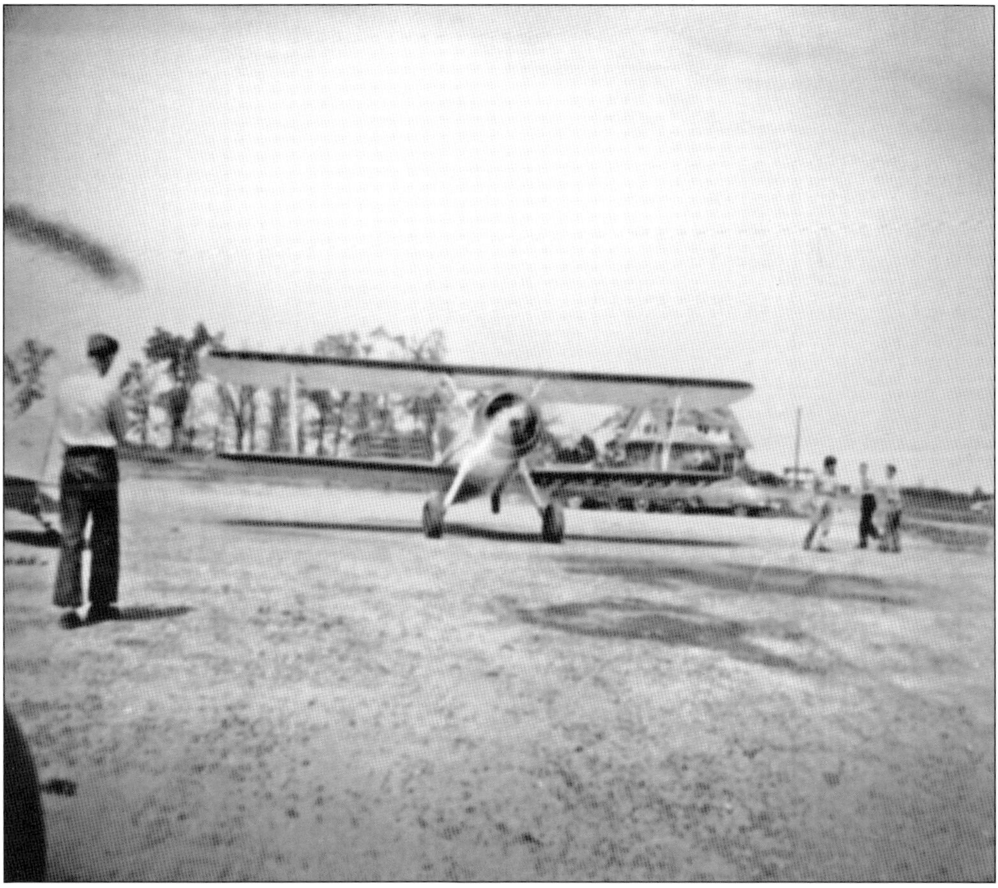

On December 17, 1903, Orville and Wilbur Wright flew their first airplane. Soon Ben Epps, who had a bike shop in Athens, Georgia, started experimenting with his own airplane. By 1919, he started the Rolf-Epps Flying Service with his friend Monte Rolfe. From the appearance of the propeller and blowing dust, the pilot of this WACO cabin plane is either making his pre-takeoff power and ignition magneto check, or actually starting to take off.

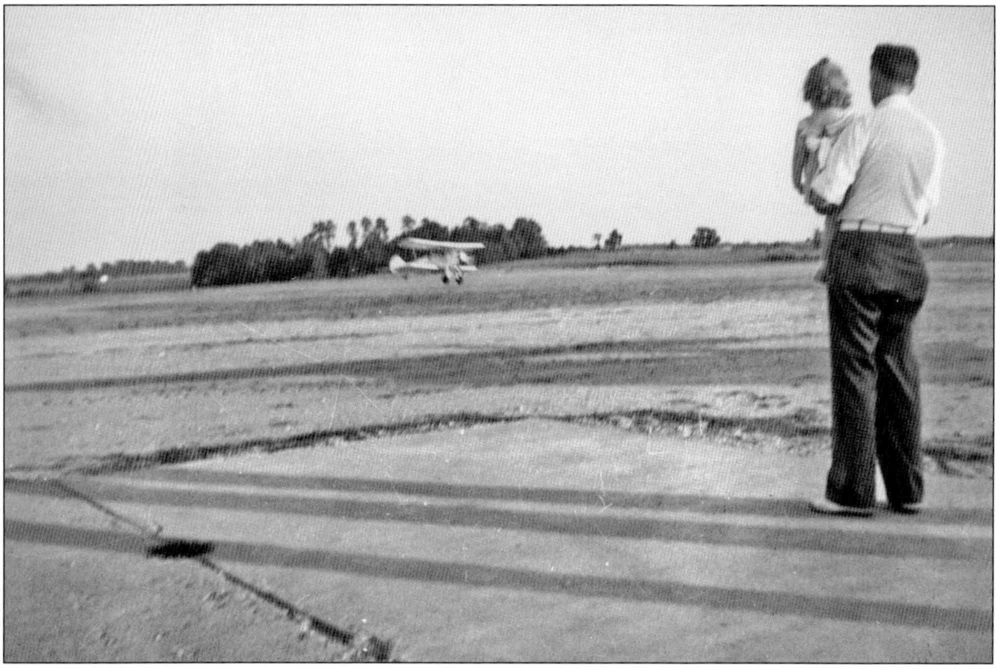

An active airfield almost always has spectators watching planes as they take off and land. The biplane seen here is possibly a Stearman. The Model 75, created in 1934, was the most popular Stearman and was primarily used as a training aircraft for the US military during World War II.

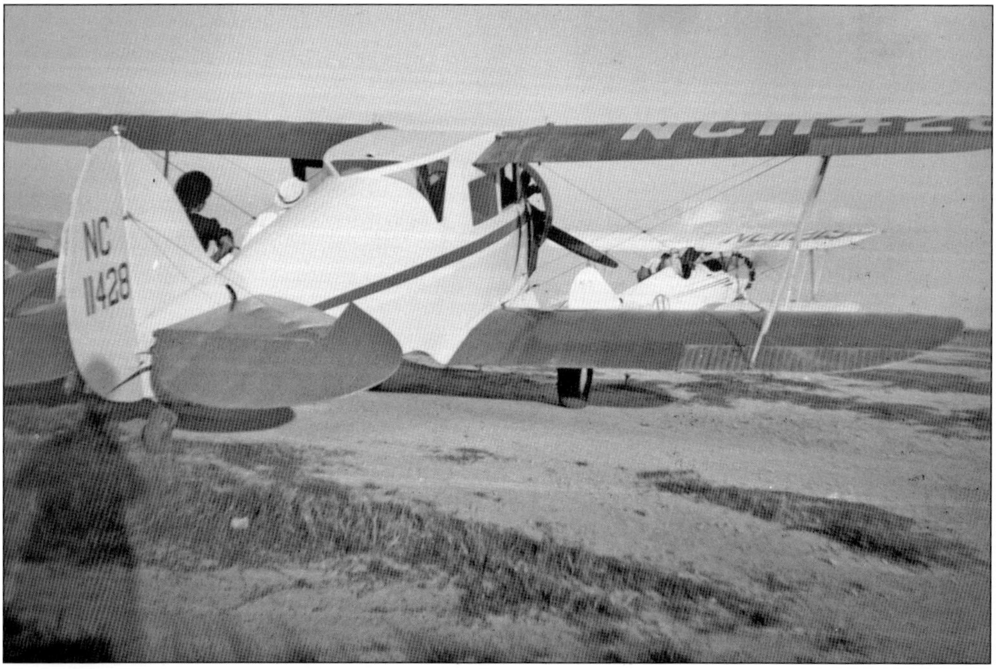

Two aircraft are queuing for takeoff. The lead plane appears to be a Stearman PT-17 trainer (another name for the Model 75). The second is a WACO four- or six-seat biplane. The runway is hard-packed dirt. If they are well drained, dirt runways are very serviceable, economical, and easy to maintain. They remain popular for rural airports to the present day.

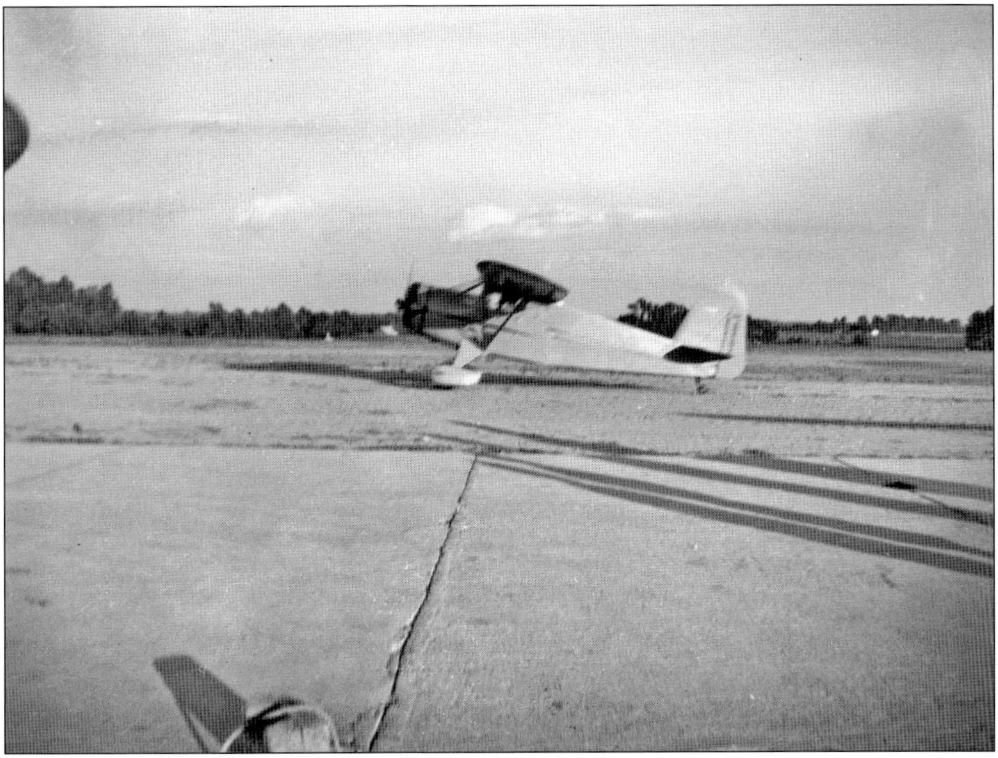

This jaunty cabin monoplane two-seater is probably a Monocoupe, a sports plane popular in the 1930s. The concrete in the foreground may be a parking or service ramp or a taxiway. The airplane appears to be poised for takeoff from a dirt airstrip.

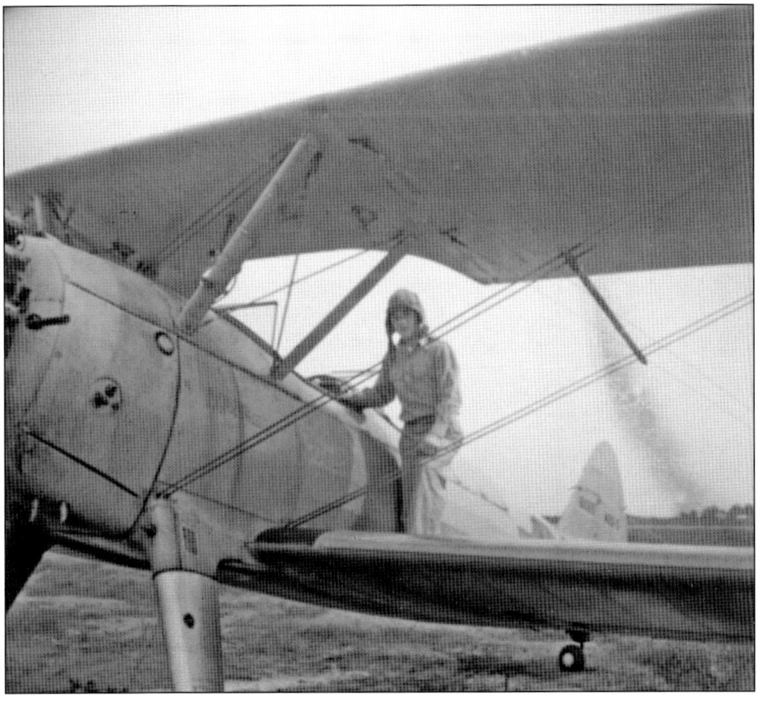

This biplane is probably a Stearman PT-17 or a WACO UPF-7, a type built in the thousands during the 1930s and 1940s and used to train World War II pilots. The young man standing on the wing appears ready to climb into the front seat, maybe for an instructional ride. The pilot was in the back seat. The canvas pull-on helmet was commonly worn in open-air cockpits.

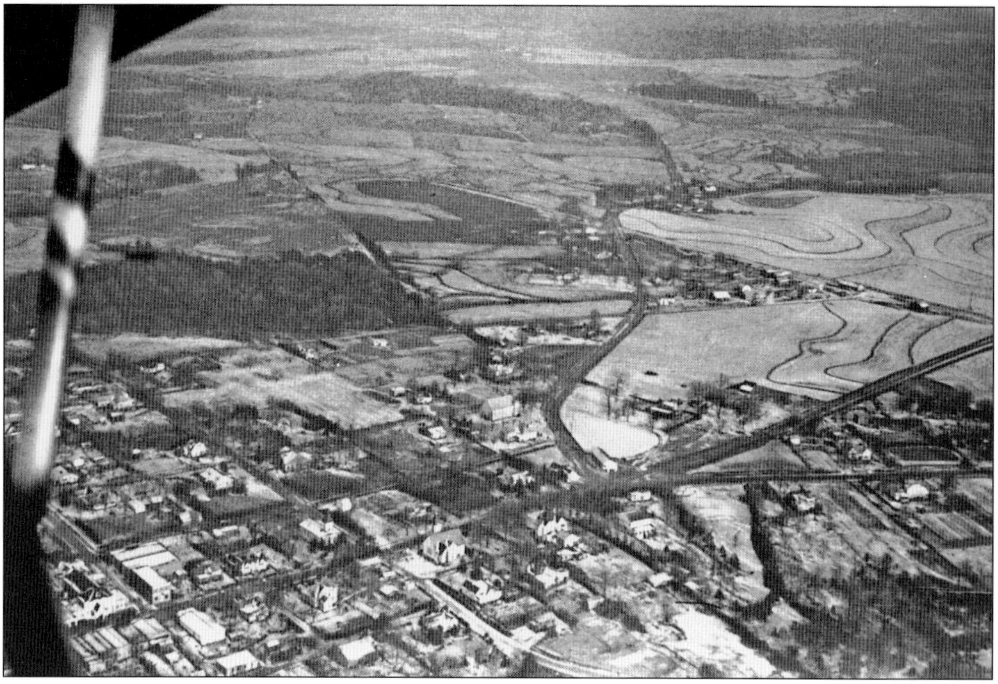

The easiest way to get oriented in this aerial view is to look for the churches. The Methodist church and Christian church are at center. The intersection of Barnett Shoals Road, Highway 15, and South Main Street is also visible. The Baptist church is on the bend of Barnett Shoals Road.

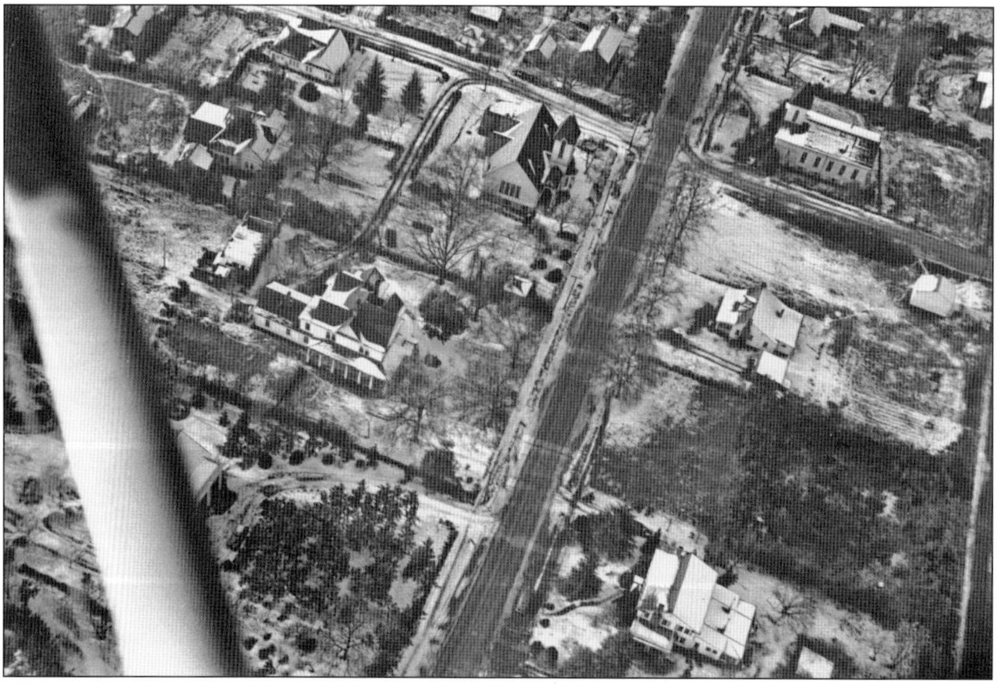

This is a close-up aerial view of Main Street with the Methodist church at top left and the Christian church at top right. The large house at center was built by Alexander Woodson "A.W." Ashford in 1893. The large house at bottom was the duplex where the Gordons lived.

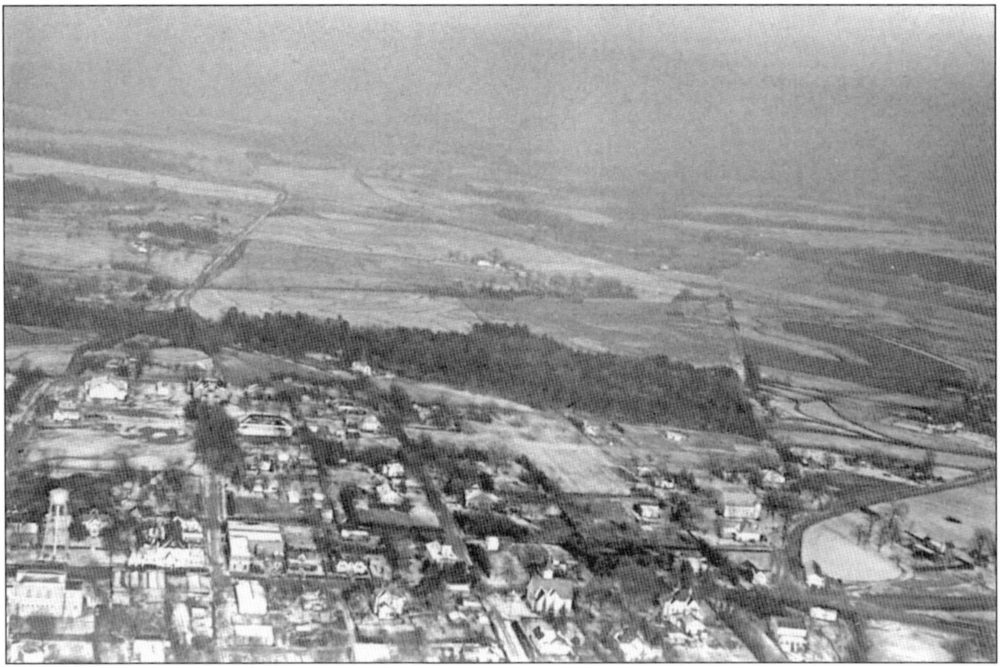

The water tower and the two churches show where Main Street is located. The largest house in the block to the left of the Methodist church is the Murray house. It was built around 1900 by Ida Murray. The high school complex is at upper left.

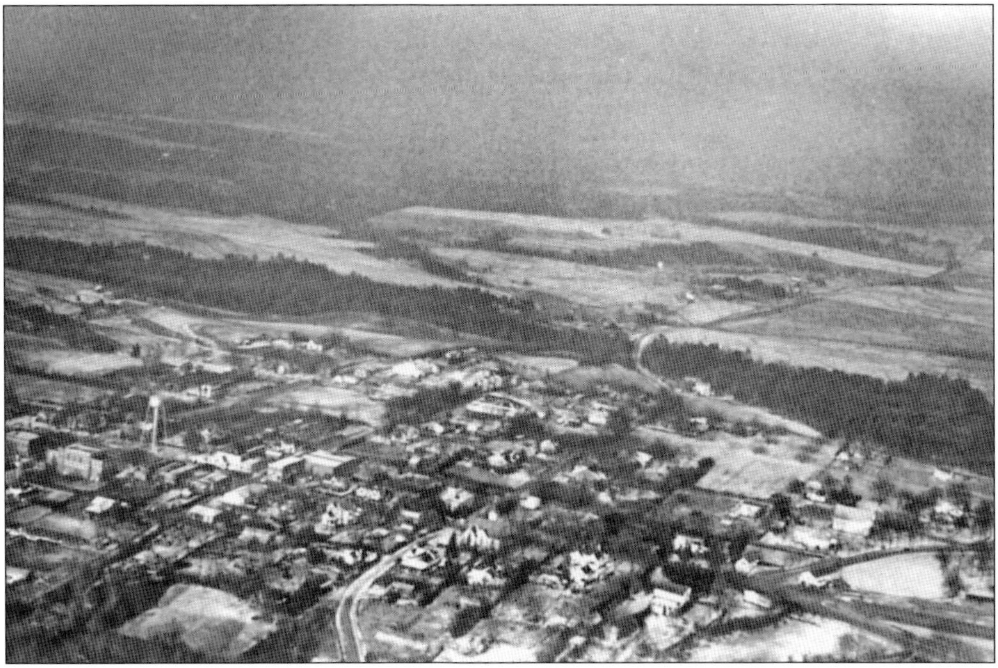

This photograph includes more of North Main Street and shows the downtown businesses. To the left of the water tower is the Eagle Tavern, and across the street is the courthouse, which was built in 1939. The previous one was destroyed in a fire in 1938. Behind the tavern is the baseball field (today called Rocket Field) and the high school complex.

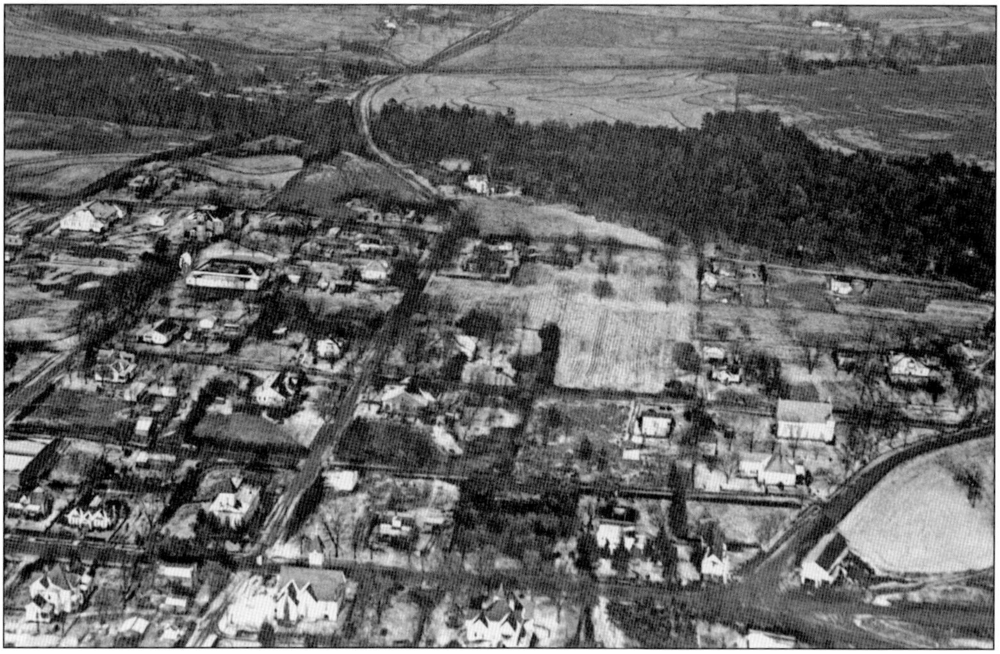

This is a closer view of the high school complex. The white buildings on the left are the agricultural complex and the cafeteria. The large brick building is the high school. Just down the street on the right is the new gym, which was started by parents in 1933 and finished using some of the first funds the US government distributed to give people jobs during the New Deal.

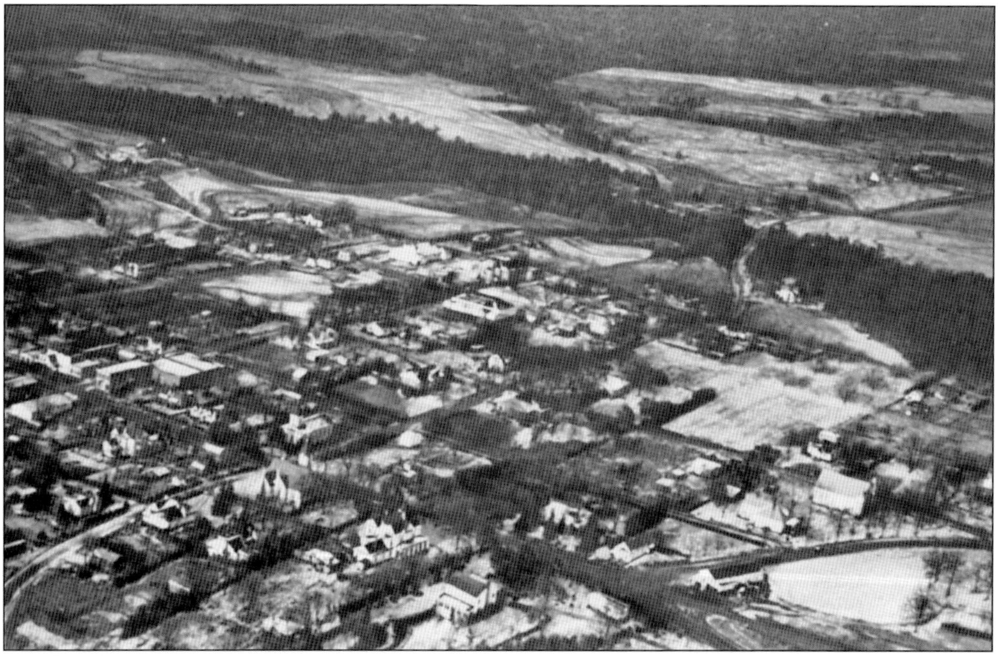

The home at the bottom of this photograph is R.E. Fain's; many of the photographs in this book were taken here. The two buildings on either side of the intersection nearby were general stores. Spec Downs operated the one on the left. The one on the right was the McRee & Company store. The Baptist church is on the corner of Barnett Shoals Road and Second Street.

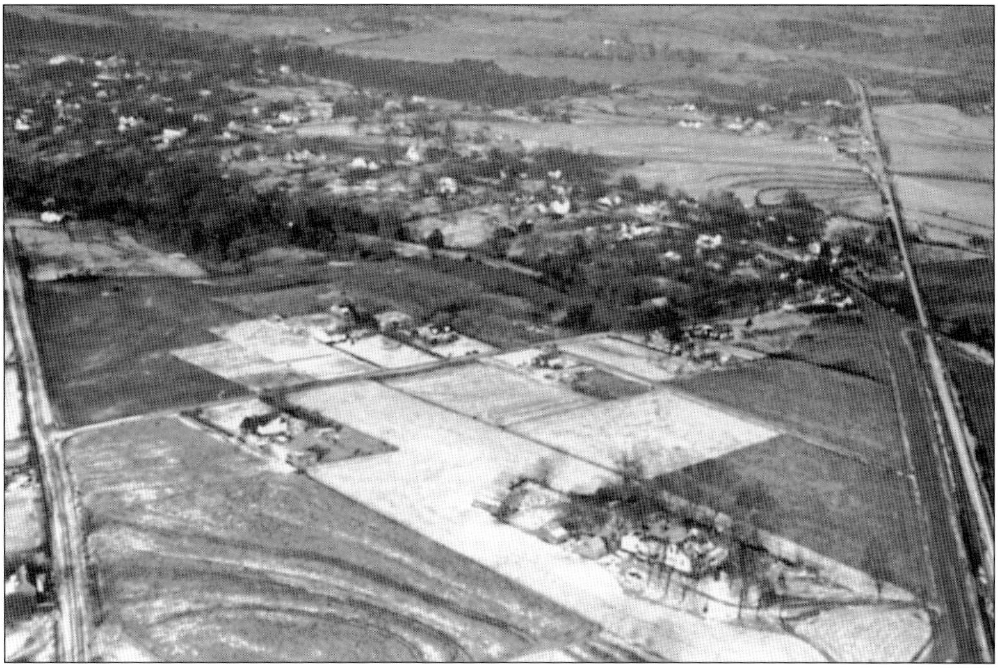

The straight line to the right is the railroad track. The depot is a small white building near the tracks at the top. Notice the agricultural lands that surrounded the town. The large house at lower right is today on the west side of New High Shoals Road, surrounded by homes that were built in the early 1950s. It belonged to William Walker Whitehead.

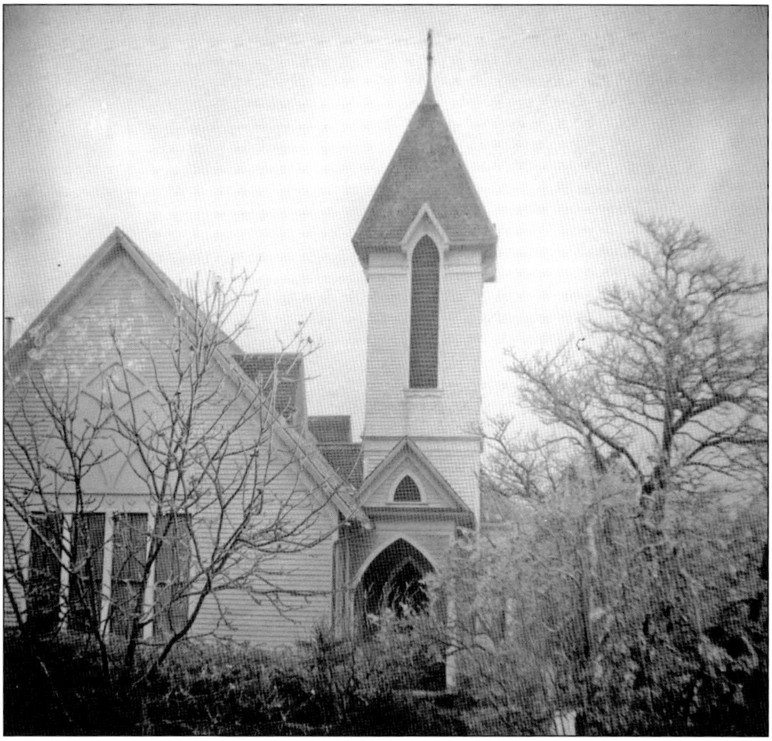

The Watkinsville Methodist Church was organized in 1802. This building, which was built by A.W. Ashford in 1893, was the fourth location of the church. This photograph was taken from the yard of the nearby Ashford home south of the church building.

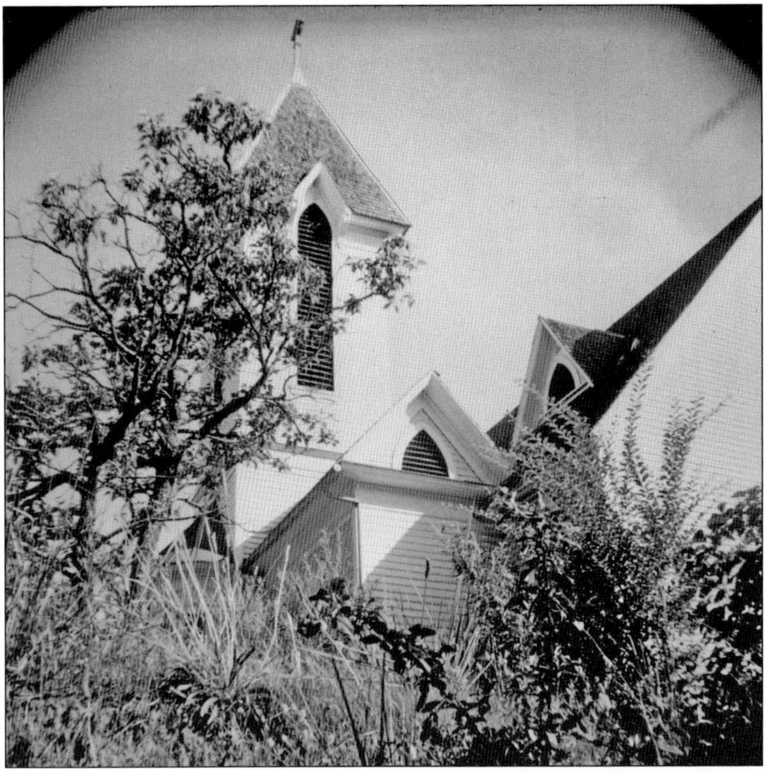

This church still stands on Main Street and is known today as the Ashford Methodist Church. This side view of the church was taken from the northern side of the building. In 1935, church members dug out a basement underneath the building. Digging was done by hand until it was deep enough to bring in a mule.

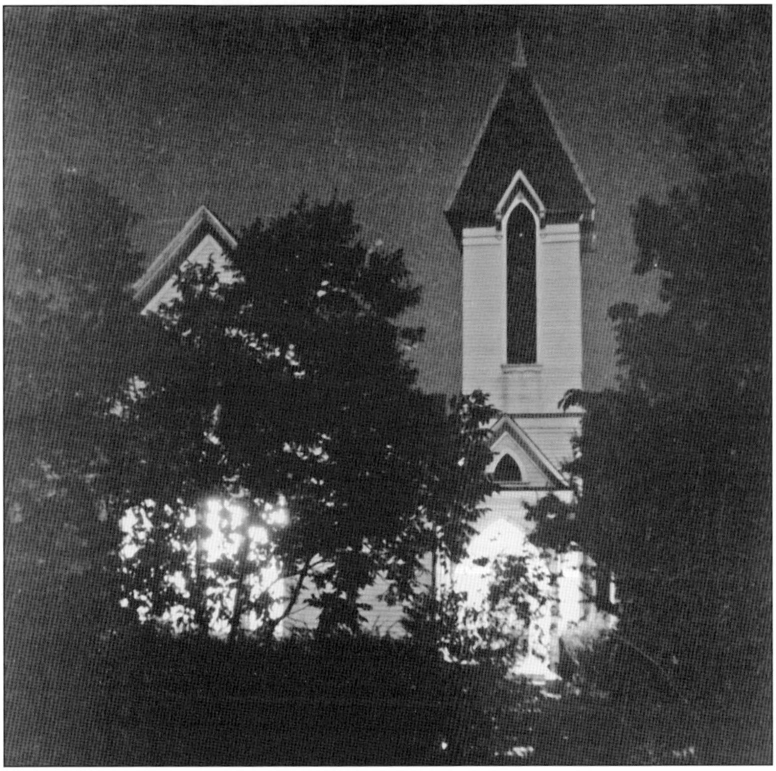

This nighttime view of the front of the church was taken from across the street at the previous location of the church. That building became the Watkinsville Christian Church when this church was built.

This grocery store was in the building that is now the home of the Elizabeth Ann Florist shop. The building across the street that is reflected in the window was originally A.W. Ashford's store and opened in 1898.

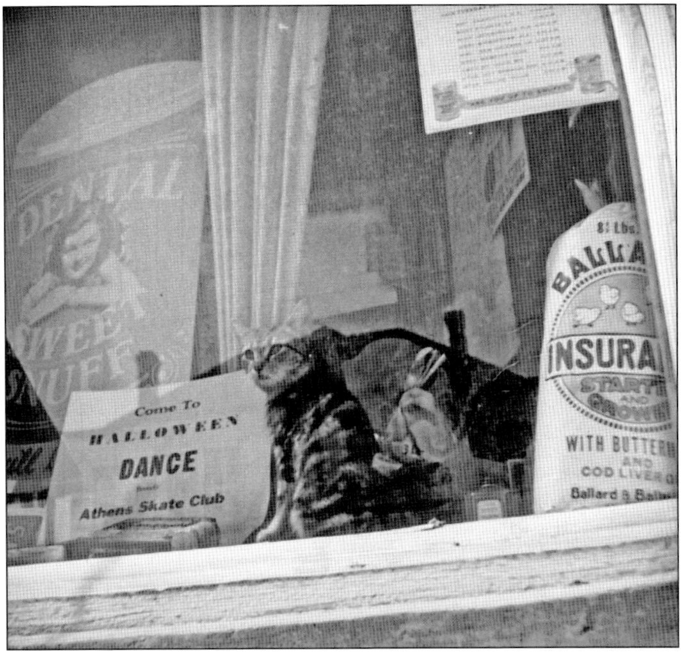

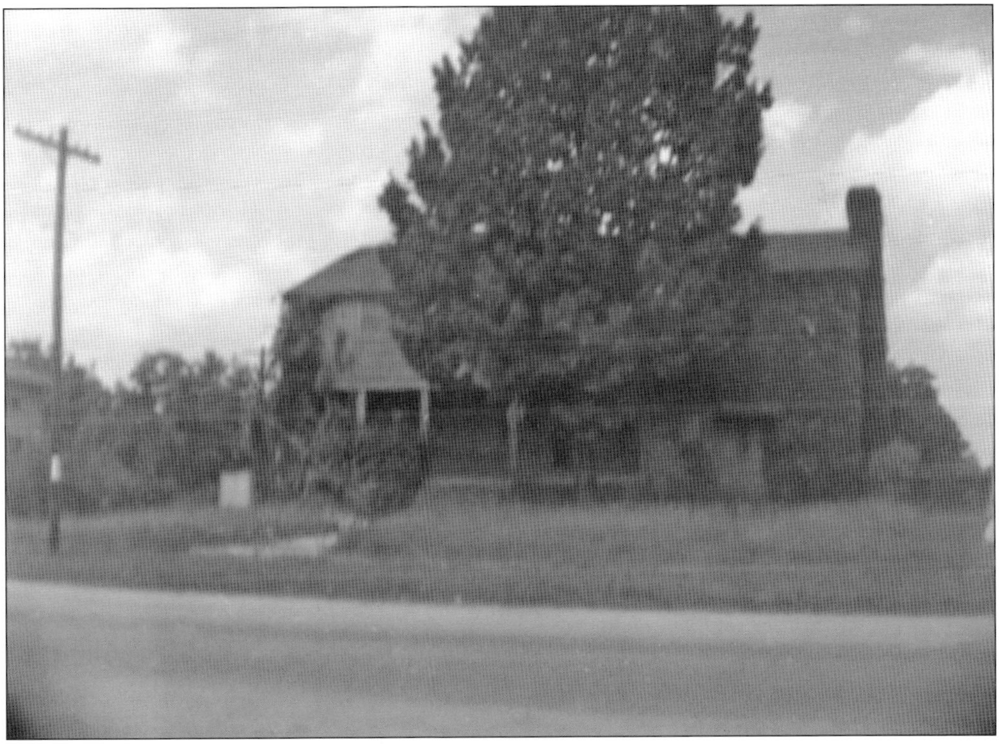

One of the oldest buildings in Watkinsville is the Eagle Tavern. By 1802, when the town was established, there was a tavern. Watkinsville was on the main stage route from Milledgeville north, and the tavern was built to serve travelers. Over the years, the tavern was expanded, so that when these photographs were taken, there were 17 rooms on several different levels with three staircases.

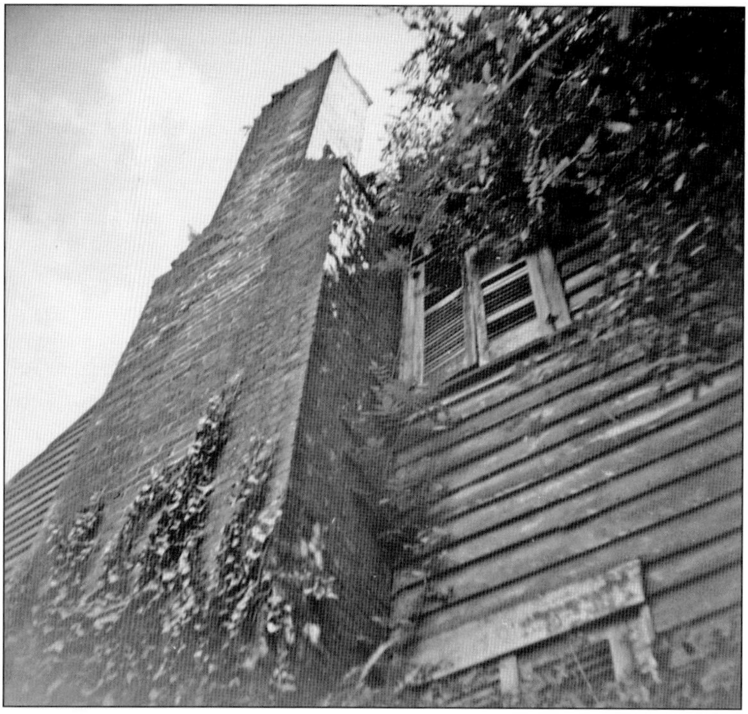

This is a close-up view of the tavern and its chimney. Lanier Billups was the owner. Several families over the years have called the tavern home. It became a haven for temporary "war widows" during World War II. The state became the owner in the 1950s and removed the many additions. Today, the building is a tourist attraction and museum.

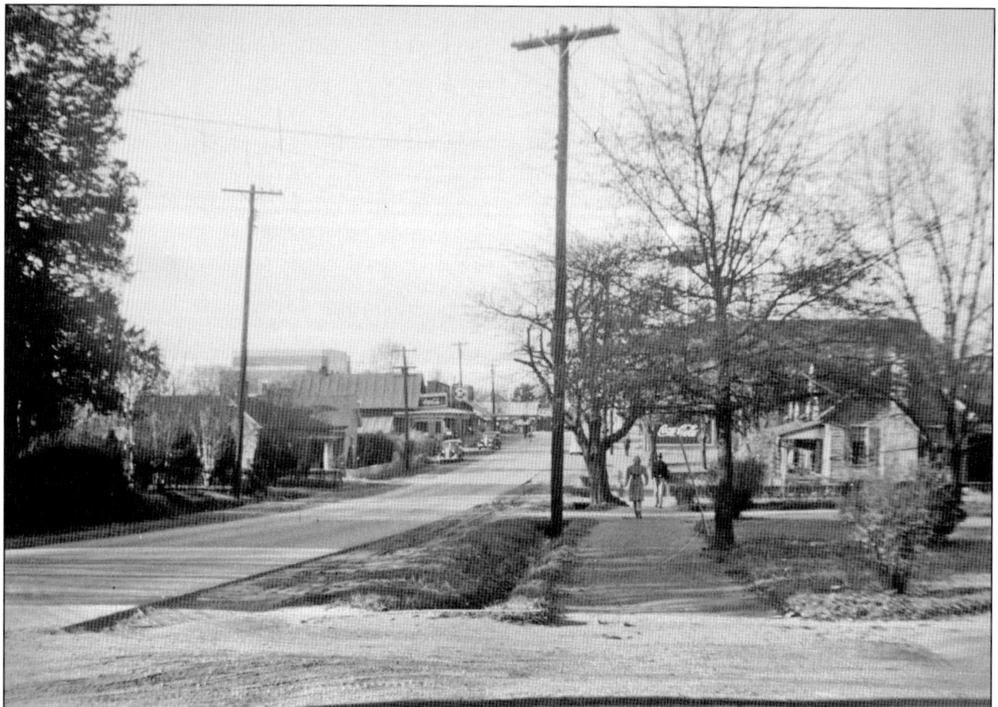

This photograph of Main Street was taken from the corner of Symington Bridge Road. The first house on the right is the old Gordon home. The top of the new (1939) courthouse is visible above the business buildings on the left side of the street.

This view of Main Street was taken north of the previous photograph and from the opposite side of the street. The buildings were constructed by A.W. Ashford in the 1920s. In the 1940s, the building closest to the water tower was Jack's radio shop. The gas station was managed by Robert Ashford.

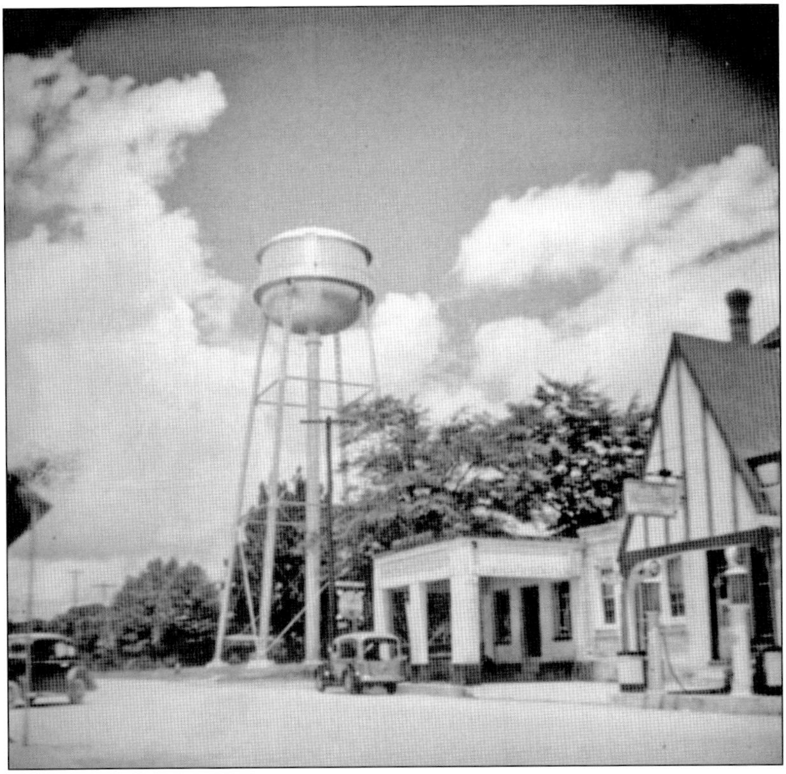

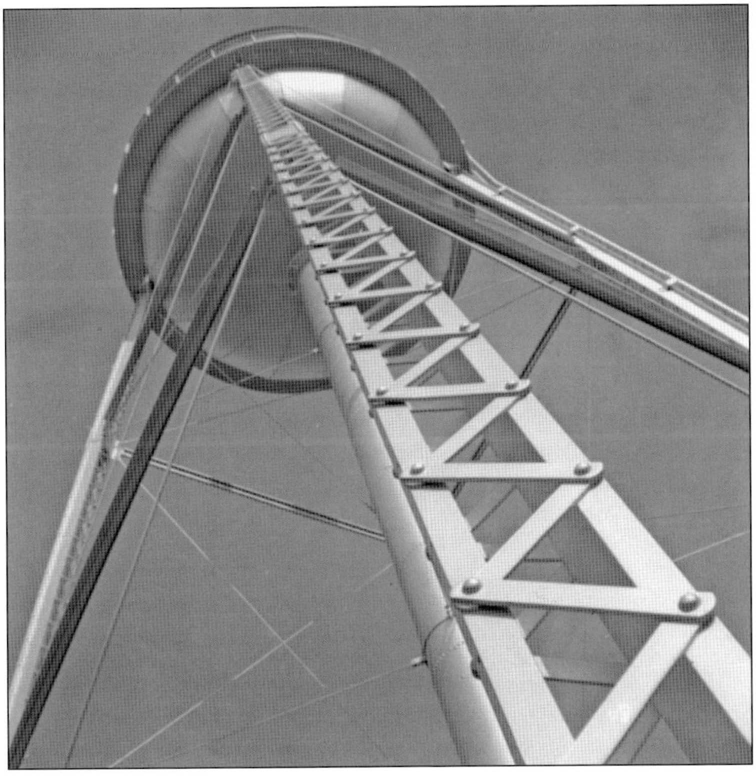

In 1938, the town of Watkinsville voted for bonds to install a modern water system. The plant, which was operated by Lamar Clark, was on Highway 53 along Calls Creek. The water tower, which was a prominent landmark in downtown Watkinsville until it was taken down in the 1990s, was also part of the system. It was near the Eagle Tavern.

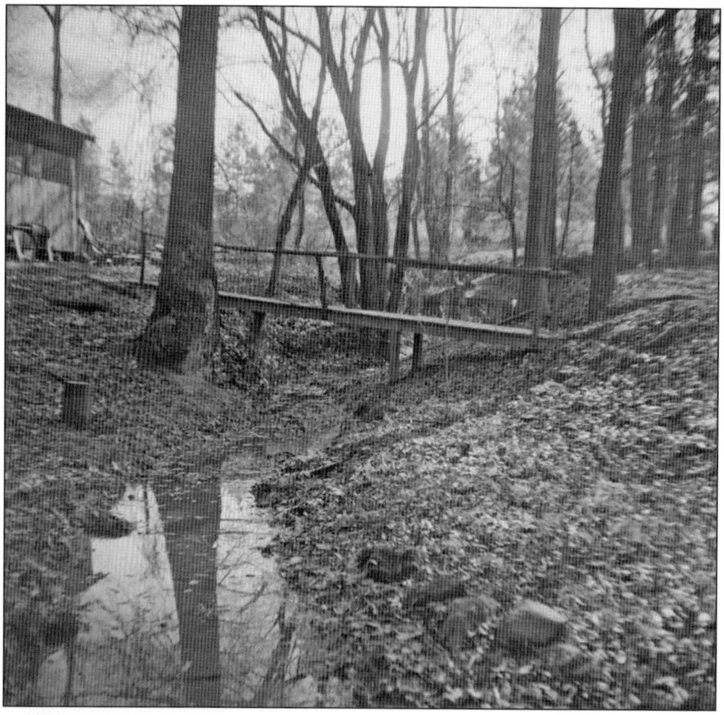

South of the Fain home was an open area with a small creek. Today there are houses along the street, but behind them, the little creek is in an area known as Watkinsville Woods.

This section of Calls Creek is known as Harris Shoals. The Hershel Harris family deeded the area to the town of Watkinsville in 1947 for use as a park and picnic area.

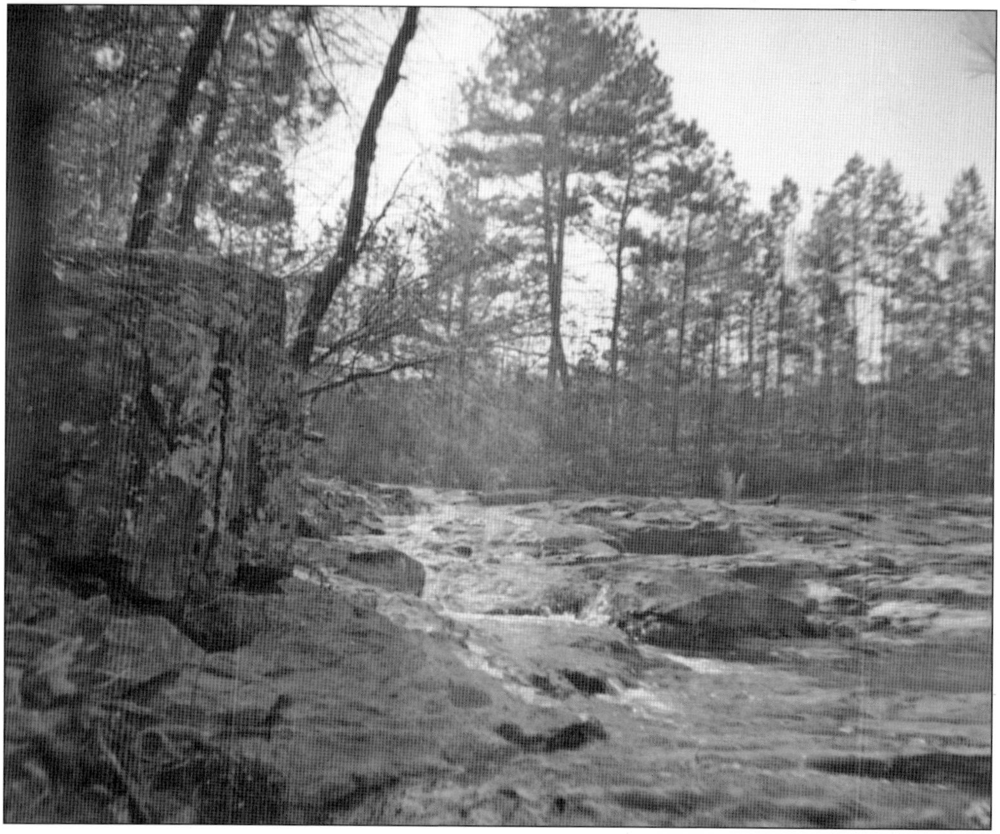

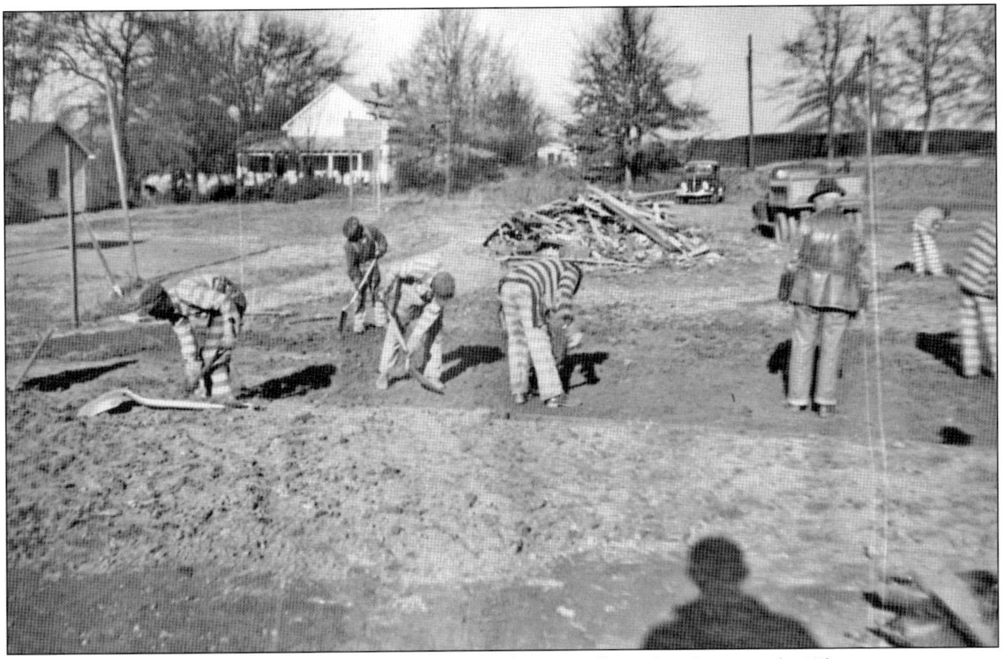

This photograph of a convict work crew was taken on the school grounds. The convicts were assigned to the county by the State Board of Prisons and Patrols in Atlanta. Reuben Jacob McGuire was the warden. The home in the background was built in 1883 as the Watkinsville Baptist Church. In 1907–1908, the church moved to the corner of Third Street and Barnett Shoals Road, and this became someone's home.

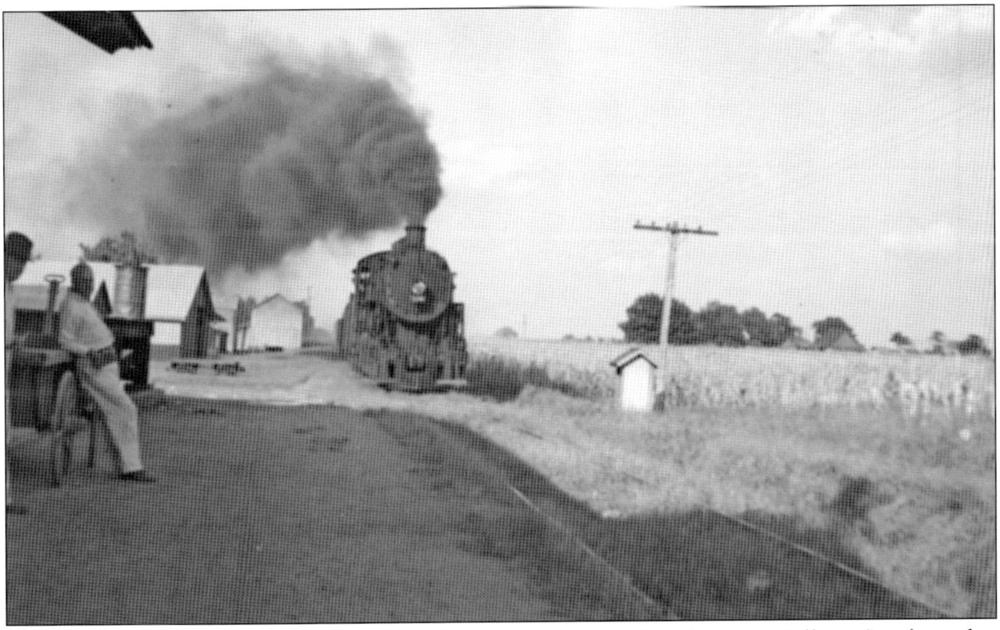

The Watkinsville depot was built in 1903. It was a gathering place for townsfolk on Sundays after church. While people were waiting for the train, young couples would walk the rails, and the younger ones would place pennies on the tracks so the train would flatten them when it arrived. People rode the train to Athens on Saturdays to shop and attend the movies.

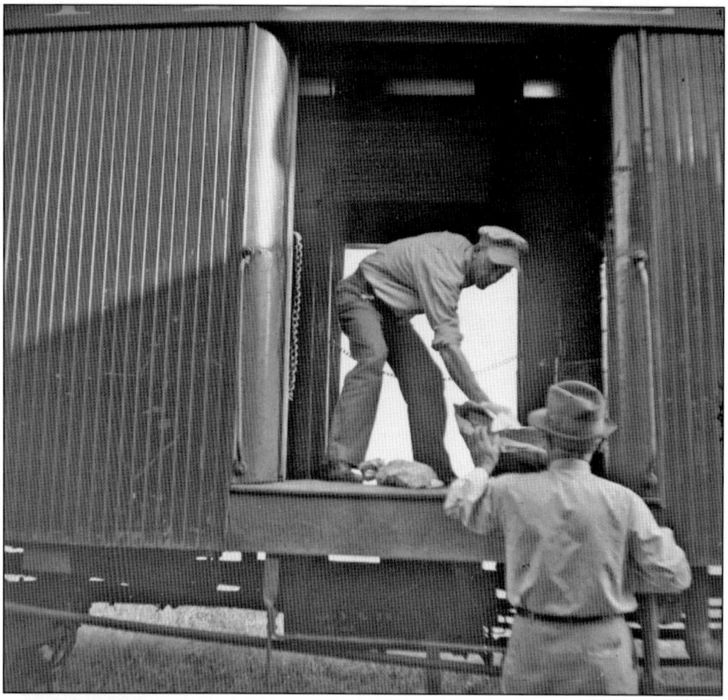

Two men are unloading a train. Before the arrival of the railroad, mail was delivered to town three days a week. Once the trains started running, the mail arrived daily.

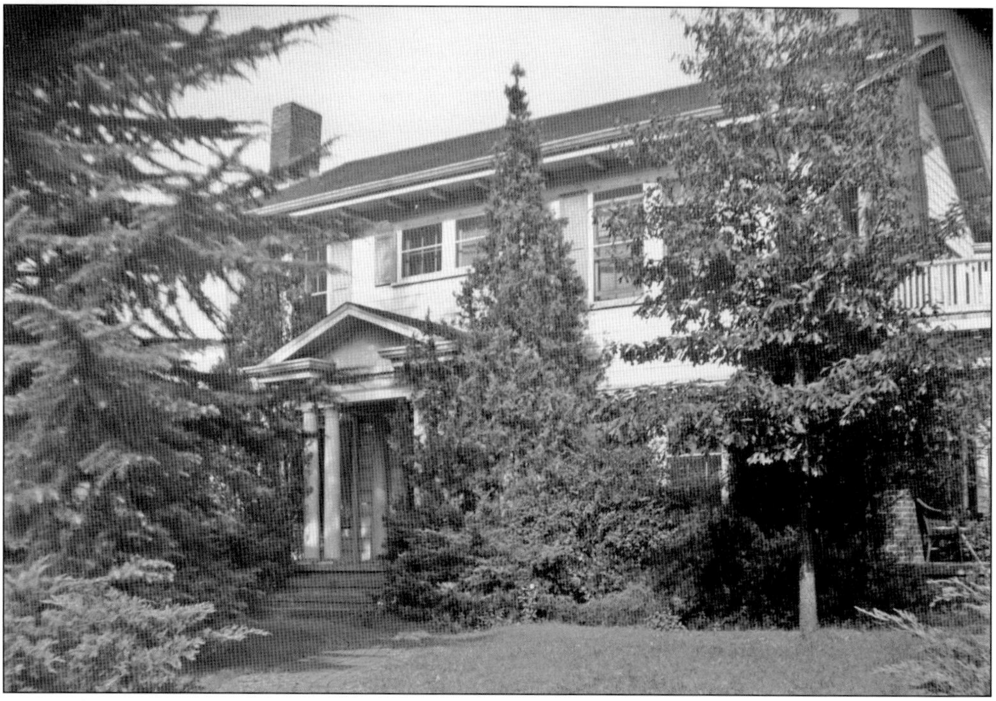

Around 1900, this was known as the Langford house because W. Bedford Langford and his wife, Ellie, lived here. In the 1930s, Russell Edward "R.E." Fain bought the house and remodeled it, turning it into a duplex. Hugh and Mary Gordon and their four children lived here at the time these photographs were taken. The duplex was acquired by Mike Todd and moved to Winterville in Clarke County in the spring of 2003. It stood where today's Town Center shopping center is.

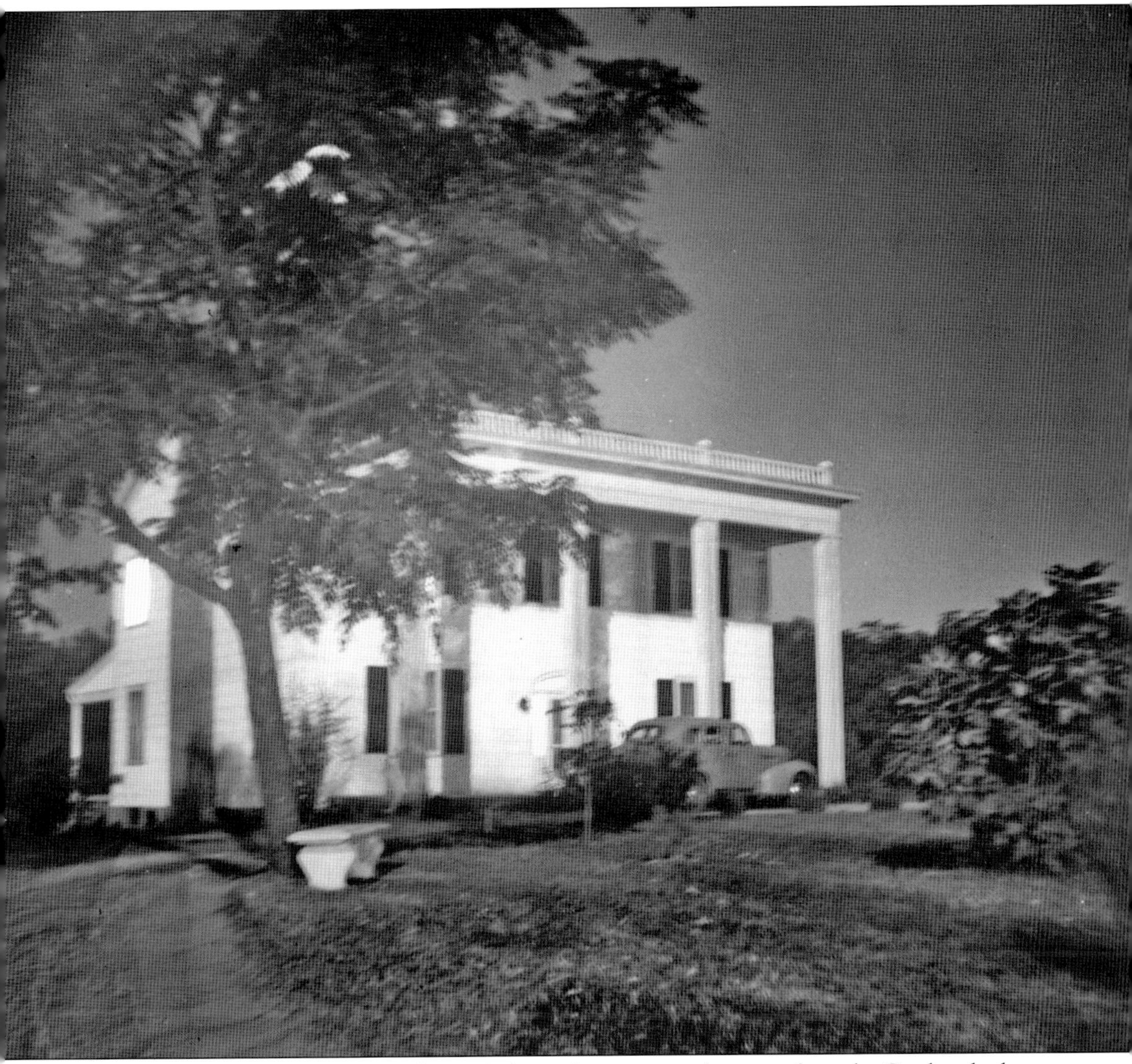

Around 1900, this was the home of Kitty Jackson. It was across the street from the Gordon duplex. It had a one-story porch across the front with vines. R.E. Fain and his wife, Martha Osborne, bought it in the 1930s. The movie *Gone with the Wind* premiered in 1939, and the Fains were inspired to remove the porch, create one that reminded them of Tara, and move the home back from the street to its current location.

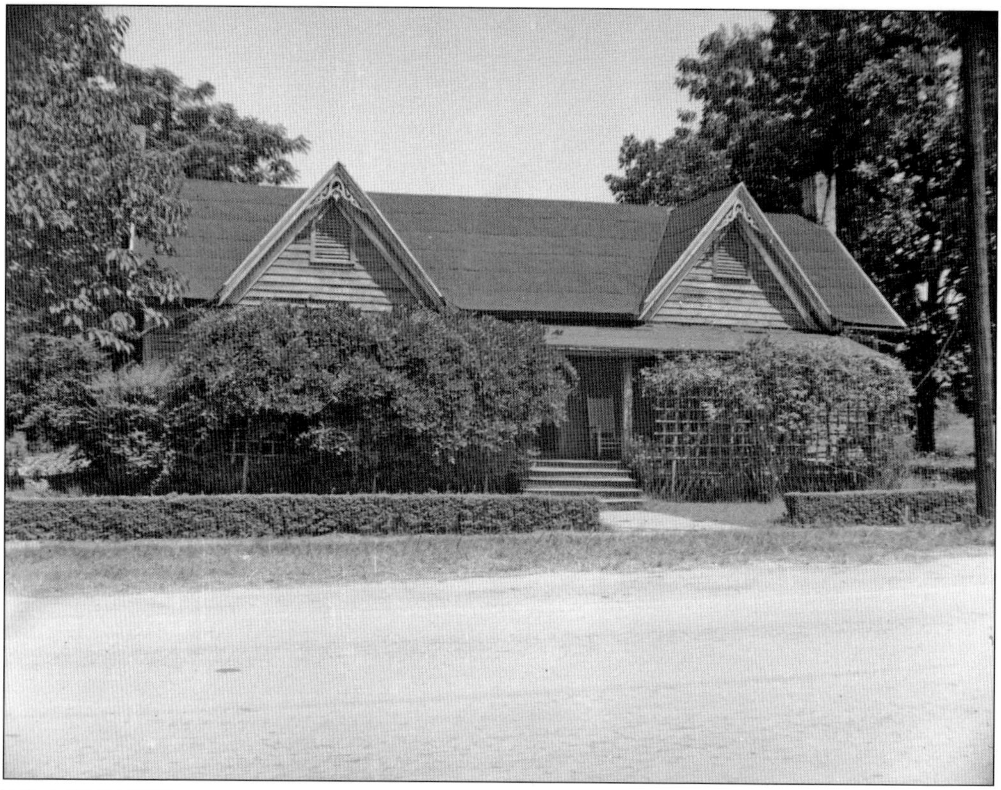

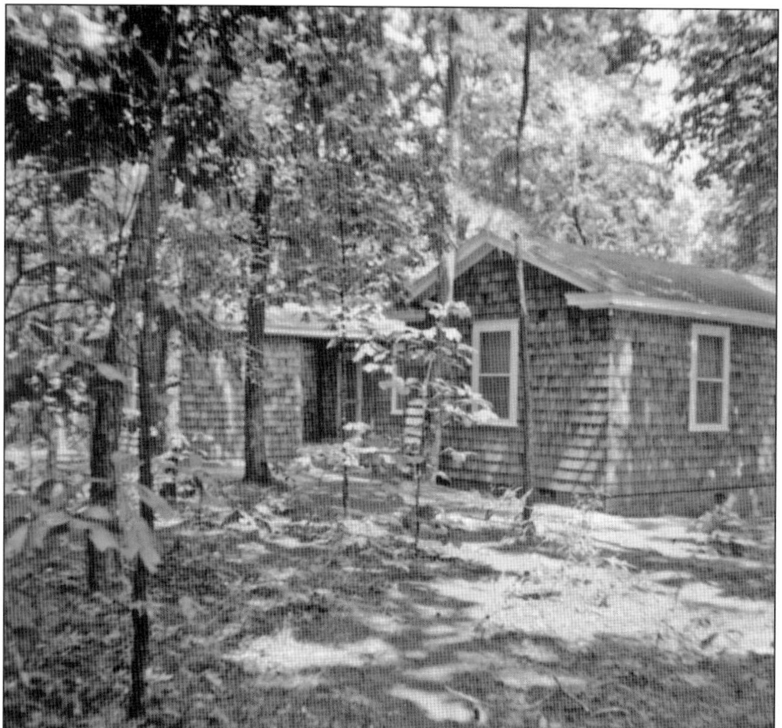

This house on Main Street was the Gordon home before they moved into the duplex. It was just north of the Christian church.

This home was on the way to the depot. It belonged to the Hargrove family, who owned the tennis court featured elsewhere in this book. Mr. Hargrove was the contractor who built Stegeman Coliseum in 1964 on the University of Georgia campus.

Two

Oconee High School

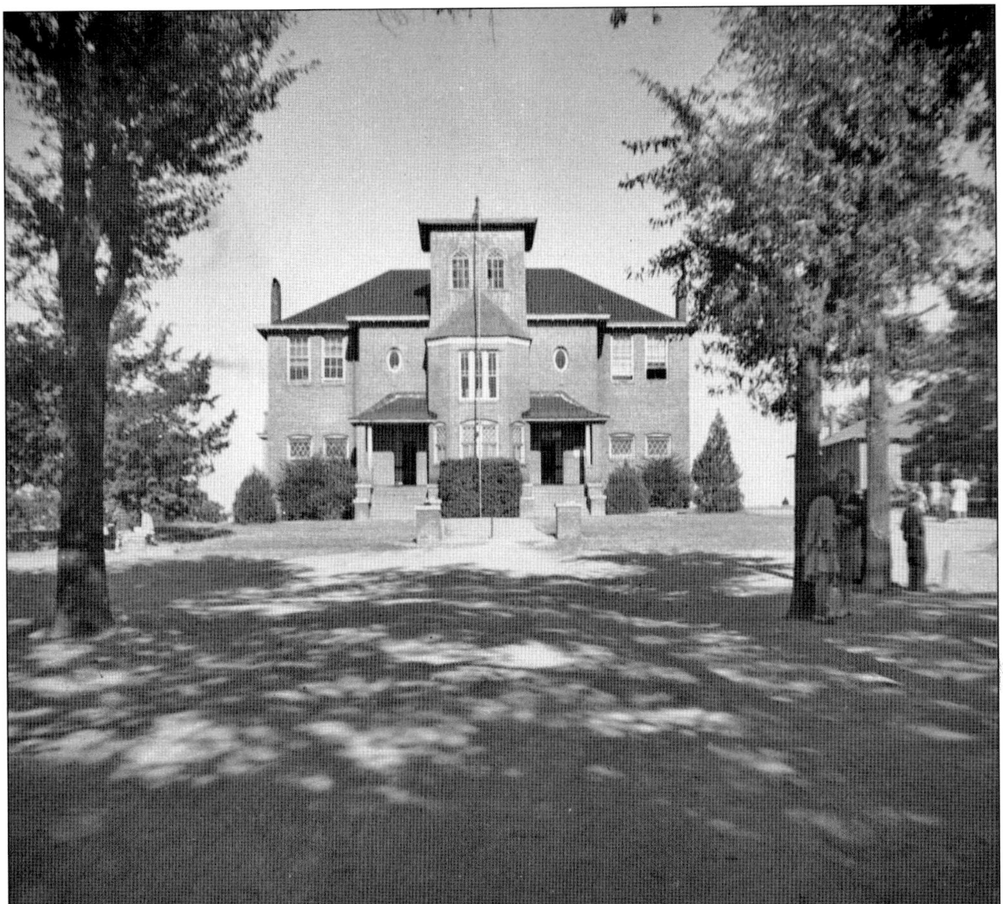

In 1902, the community organized to build a brick school building. The cornerstone reads "J.W. Johnson, mayor; Council: J.W. Butler, D.M. White, W.R. Langford, I.W. Thrasher, B.R. McRee; Board of Education: W.A. Brooks, Pres.; W.H. Ashford, Sec.; G.W. Avery; J.C. Johnson; D.A. Osborn; Architect: C.E. Choate; Contractor: C.A. Clarke; 1902." This photograph shows evidence of the major renovations that occurred in the 1920s, adding the cement steps and brick posts.

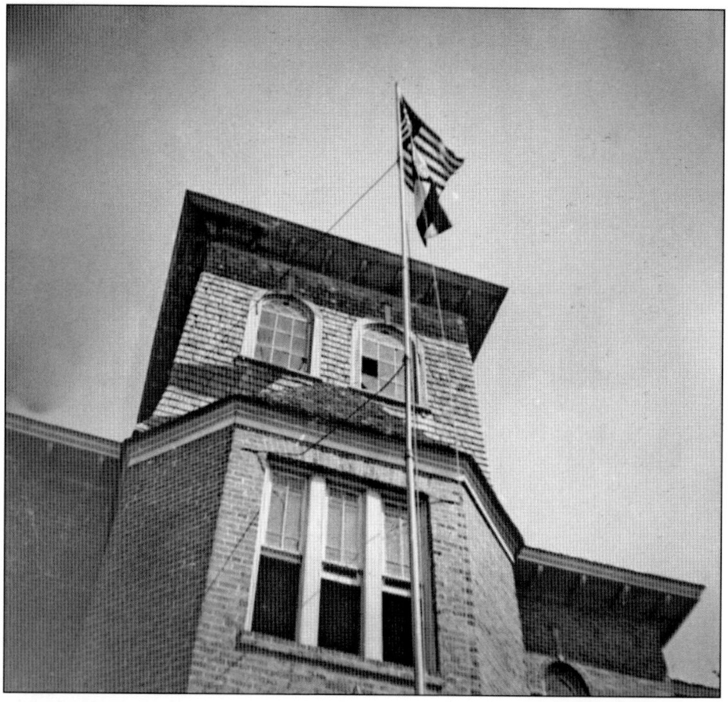

Over the years, various outbuildings such as a gym, vocational agriculture buildings, and a lunchroom were added. In 1922, a building for the four lower grades was also added. The original school building had a cupola on top of this tower. It did not last long, and most pictures of the building do not show it.

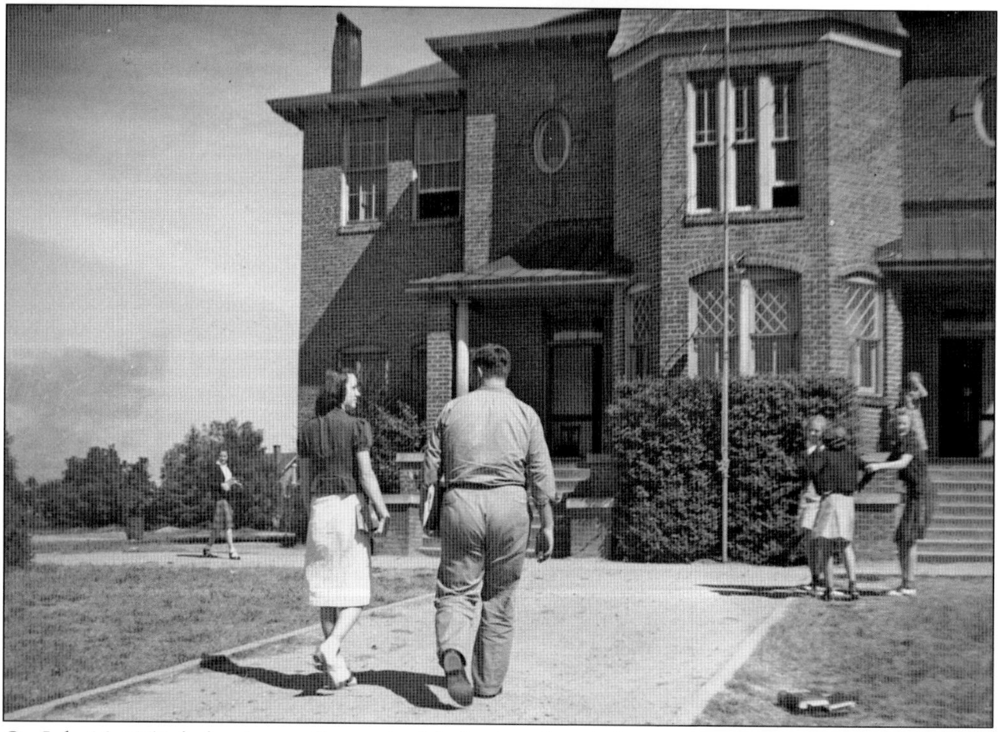

On July 16, 1954, lightning set fire to the Methodist church. Just as people were gathering to fight that fire, lightning struck the high school. It was impossible to fight both fires, so the high school suffered a lot of damage. The county was able to salvage and renovate only the lower floor of the school. Today, it is used by the Oconee Cultural Arts Foundation as an art gallery.

Students lined up by grade at the beginning of each school day and after their lunch break. This photograph was probably taken from the second-story window just behind the flagpole.

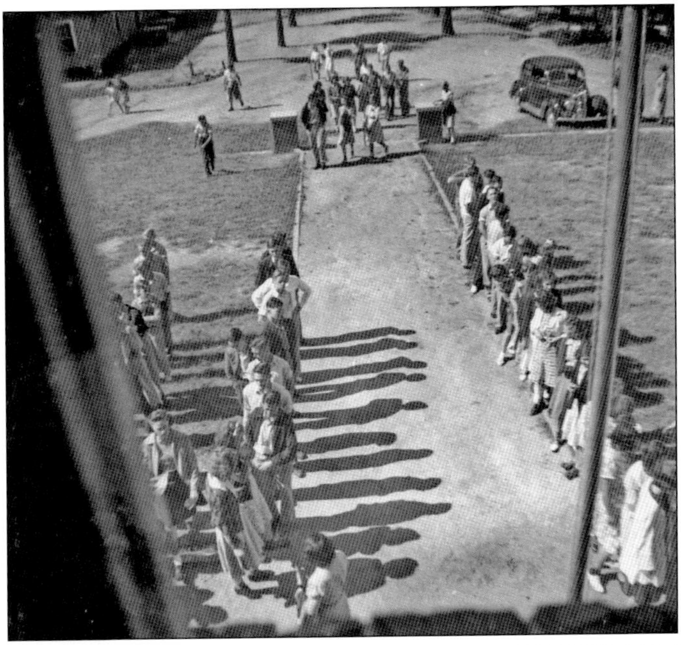

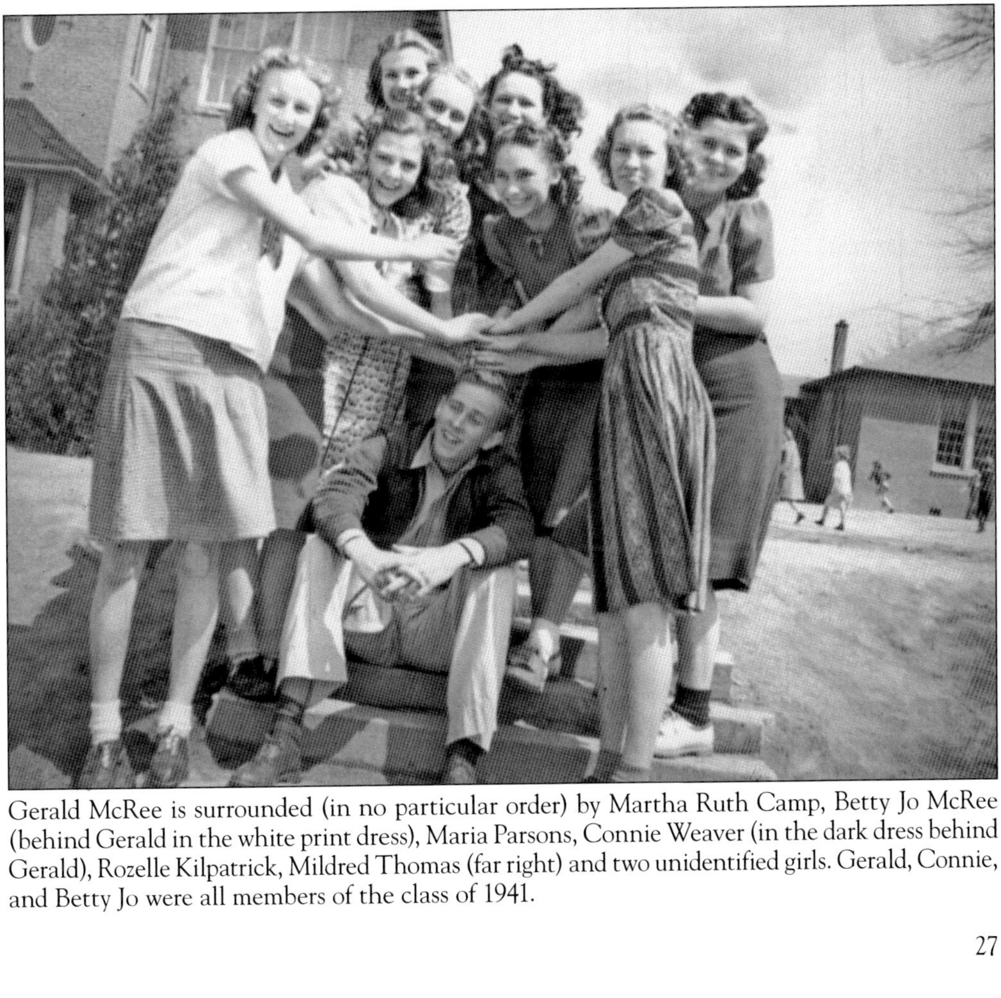

Gerald McRee is surrounded (in no particular order) by Martha Ruth Camp, Betty Jo McRee (behind Gerald in the white print dress), Maria Parsons, Connie Weaver (in the dark dress behind Gerald), Rozelle Kilpatrick, Mildred Thomas (far right) and two unidentified girls. Gerald, Connie, and Betty Jo were all members of the class of 1941.

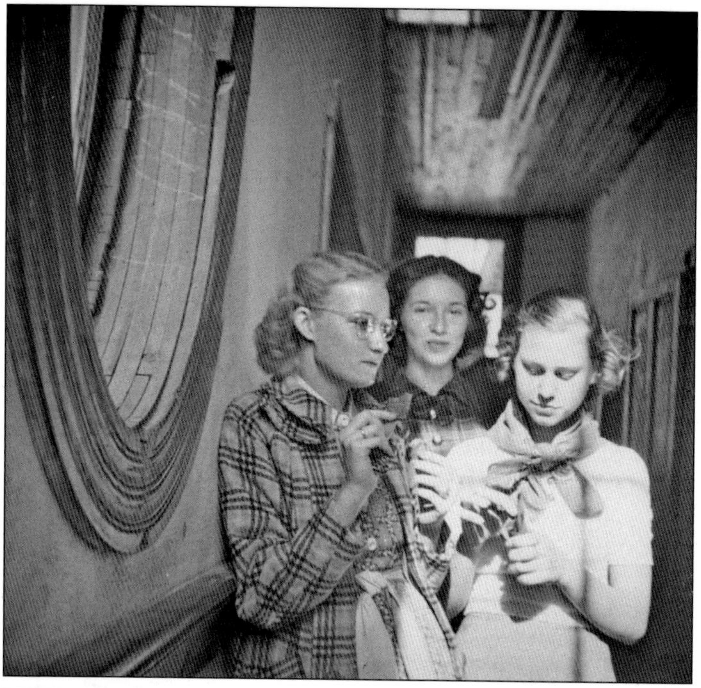

Bobby caught (from left to right) Anita Chandler, Mary Ashford, and Joan Camp taking a snack break in a hallway of Oconee High School.

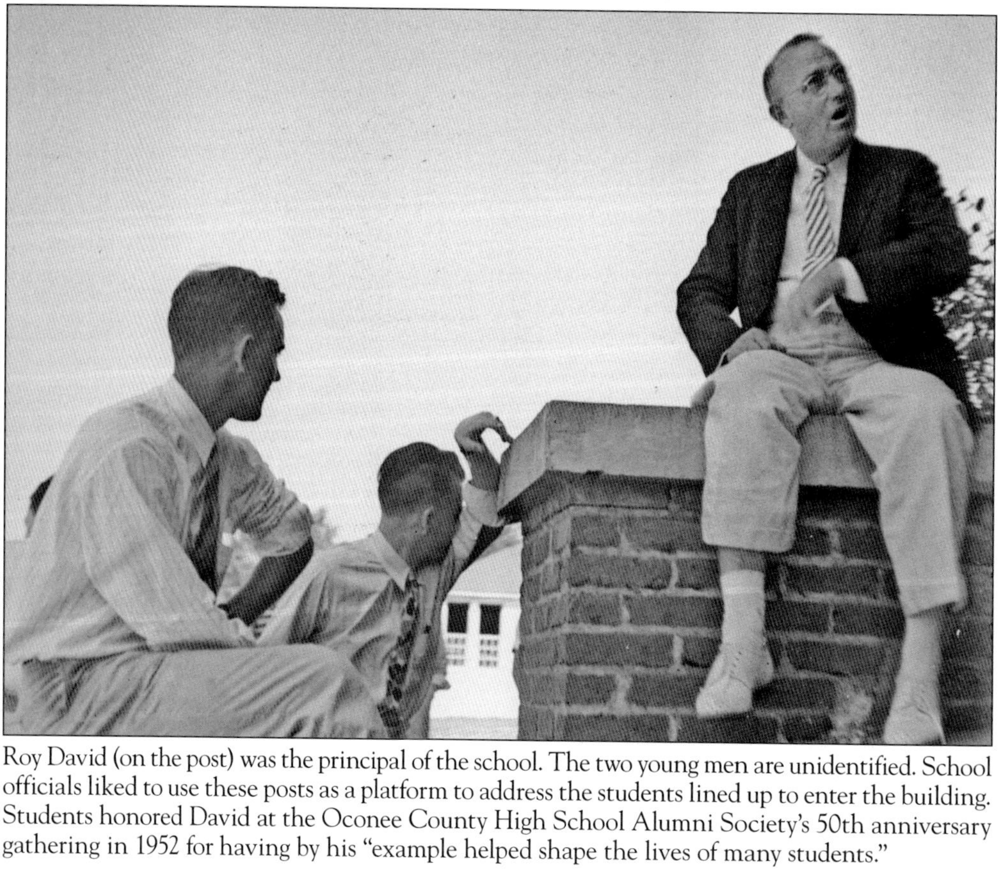

Roy David (on the post) was the principal of the school. The two young men are unidentified. School officials liked to use these posts as a platform to address the students lined up to enter the building. Students honored David at the Oconee County High School Alumni Society's 50th anniversary gathering in 1952 for having by his "example helped shape the lives of many students."

This photograph gives an excellent view of one of the classrooms. The teacher is Mrs. Ben C. Dickenson, and the student she is talking to is Grady Wheeler. One story told about her is that Chase Bishop, a student, commented that her classroom was like a car: "The crank is in the front." She replied "Maybe, but the nuts are behind."

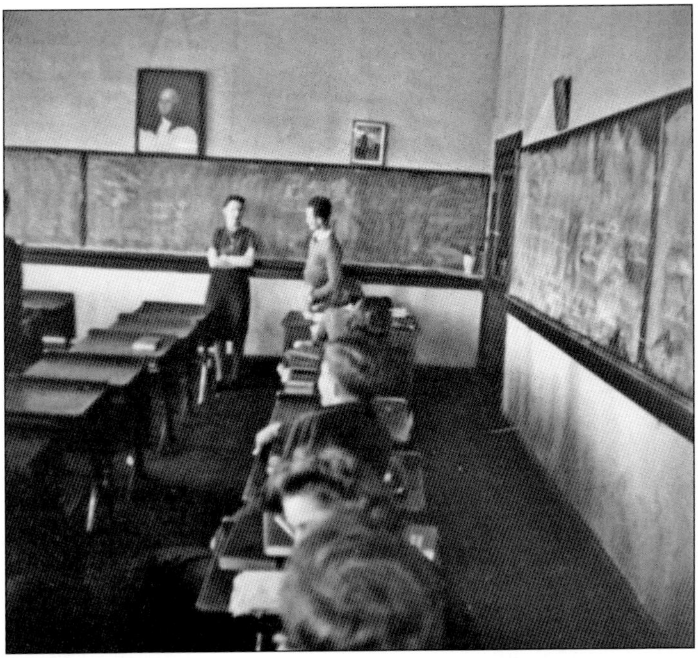

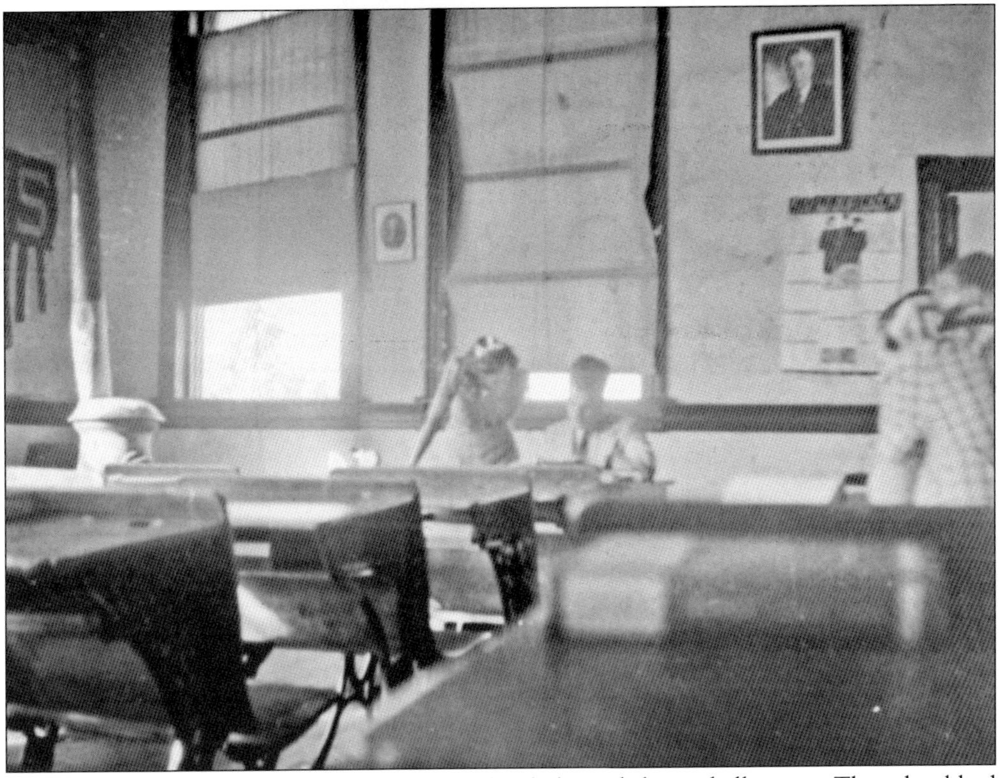

Here is another view of a classroom. Notice the desks and the potbelly stove. The school had several large classrooms like this. When one entered the front door of the school, there was a beautiful curving stairway leading upstairs. The principal's office was under the stairs in the center of the building, where he could easily keep an eye on everything.

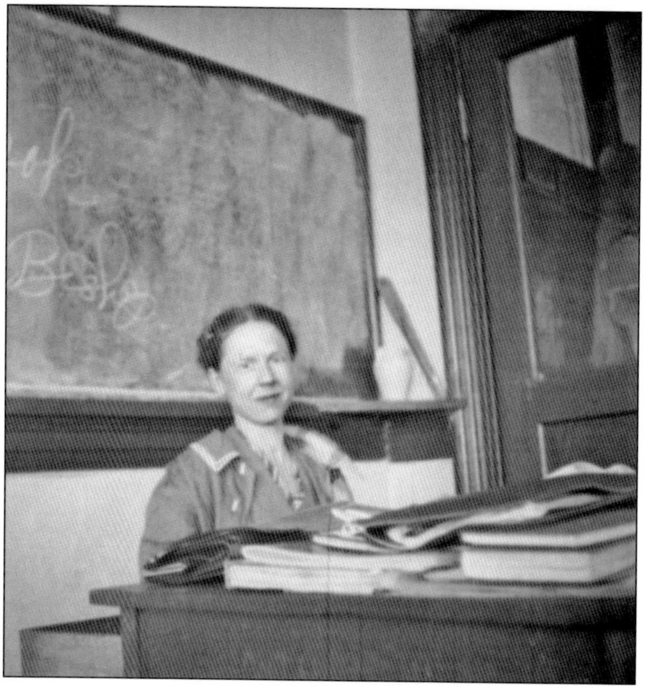

Mrs. John W. McWhorter, the teacher in this photograph, was mentioned in a 1913 article in the *Oconee Enterprise* about a party at her home organized by the 10th grade to celebrate the school's 11th anniversary. The McWhorter home was decorated in red and white for the occasion, the 10th grade class colors. According to the *Enterprise*, punch was served, games were played, adult guests gave appropriate remarks, and food was served. "Mrs. McWhorter was handsomely gowned in black satin trimmed in lace and iridescent beads," the paper reported.

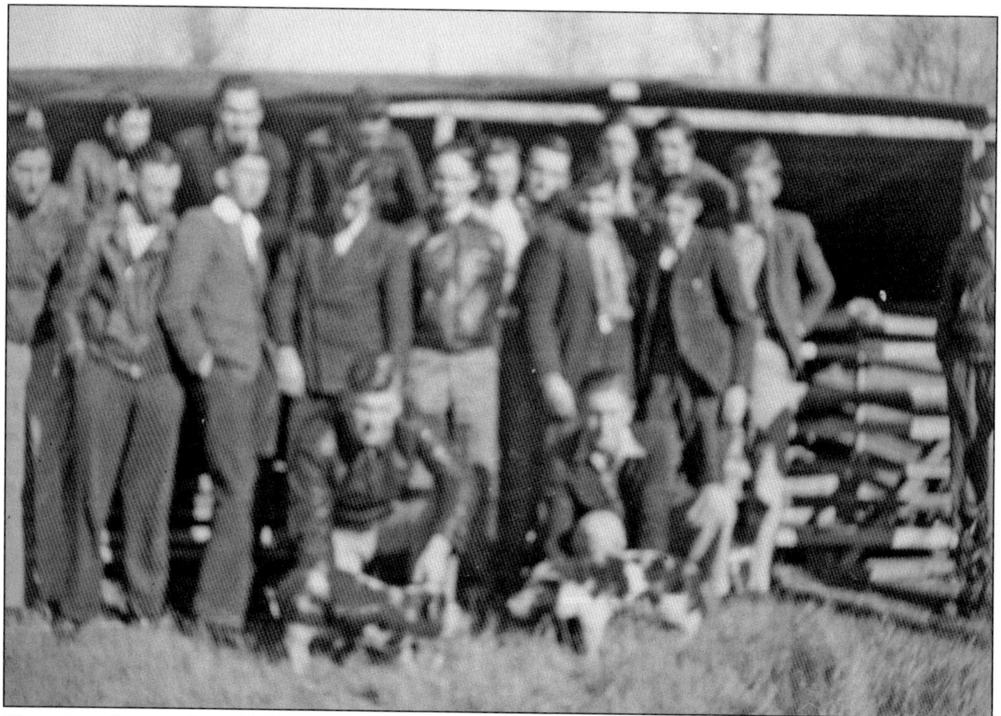

Vocational agricultural classes in Oconee County began in 1937. Future Farmers of America (FFA) members bought an incubator to hatch chicks for the community. It could hatch 3,000 chicks weekly. They pruned fruit orchards and built a barrel sprayer on a trailer so they could spray people's orchards. They used the funds earned to pay for food (oyster stew or barbecue) at meetings and to attend the summer FFA camp.

Three

Sports

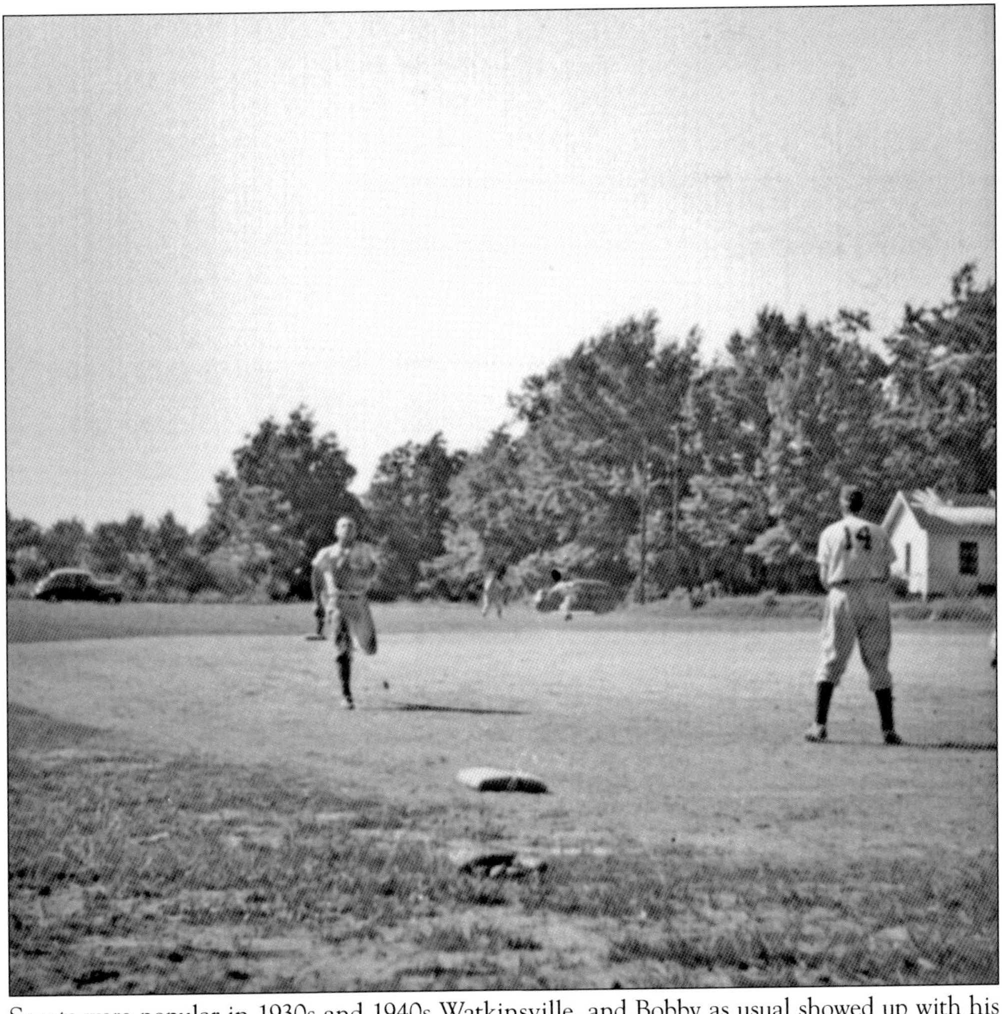

Sports were popular in 1930s and 1940s Watkinsville, and Bobby as usual showed up with his camera. The schools in Watkinsville and Bogart were big rivals. Baseball was very popular. Games were played on a field in front of the high school. The field was known as the Watkinsville School Ball Field until sometime in the 1970s, when it became known as Rocket Field after the mascot of the Watkinsville team.

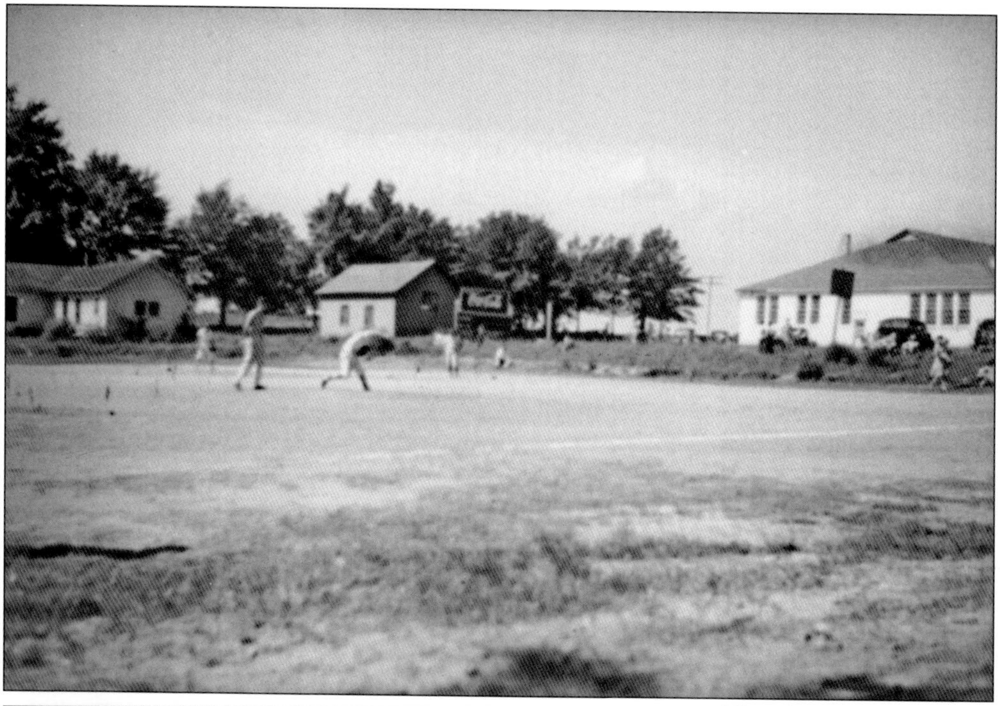

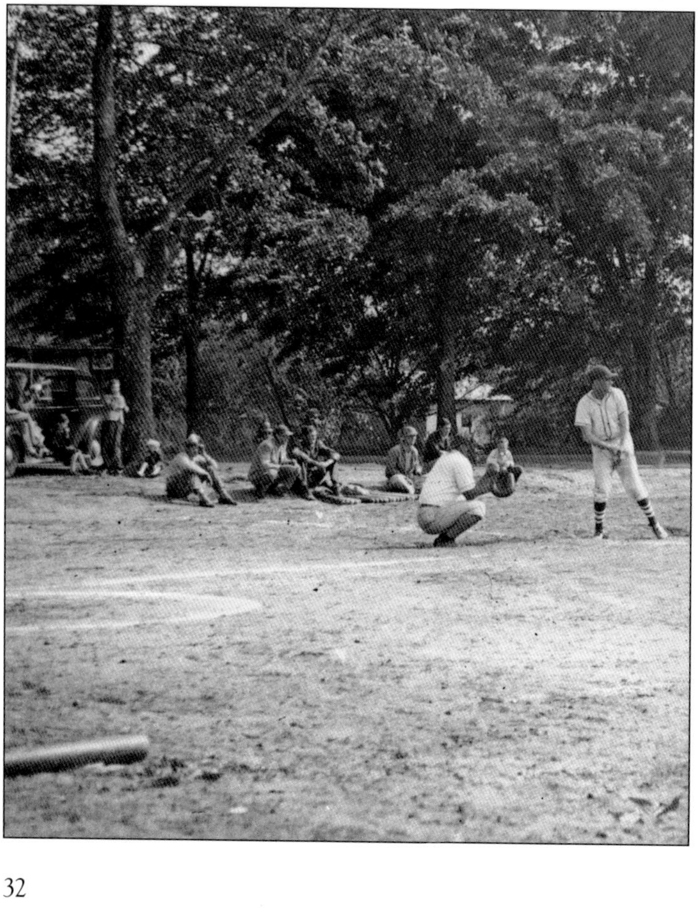

The white building at right is the cafeteria and agricultural building. In the 1980s, it was used for kindergarten classes, and today, it houses studio space for the Oconee Cultural Arts Foundation.

In addition to the school teams, local communities also organized teams. Loren and Ralph Thrasher, members of one of these teams, were good enough to try out for the majors. One of the fundraisers for the new gym in 1933 was a barbecue at Wilson's Woods with Eugene Talmadge as a speaker, followed by a double header on this field. Watkinsville played Statham, and Bishop played Commerce.

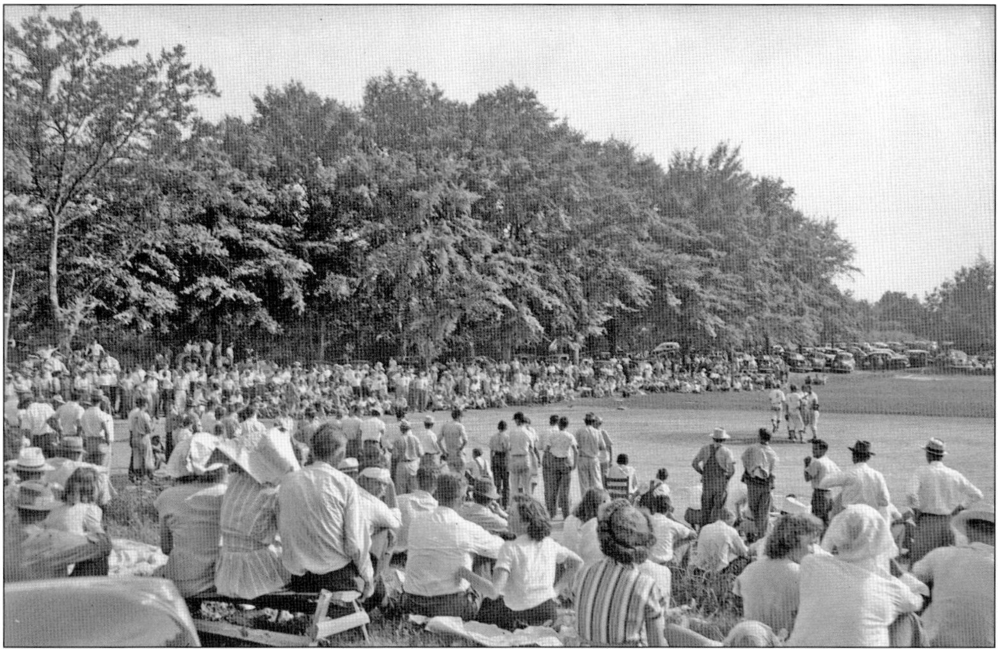

This is a view of the crowd attending one of the games. Notice the lack of stands. A few people brought their own chairs, but most brought blankets or simply stood to watch the games.

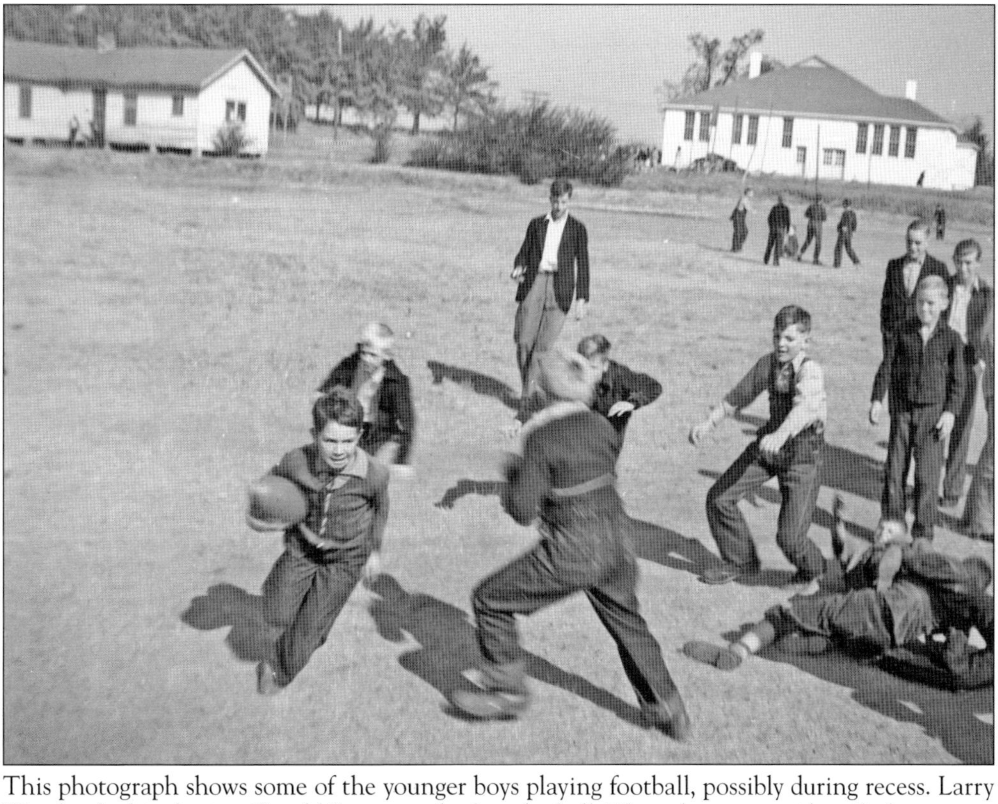

This photograph shows some of the younger boys playing football, possibly during recess. Larry Weatherford is chasing Harold Parsons, who has the ball. The others are unidentified.

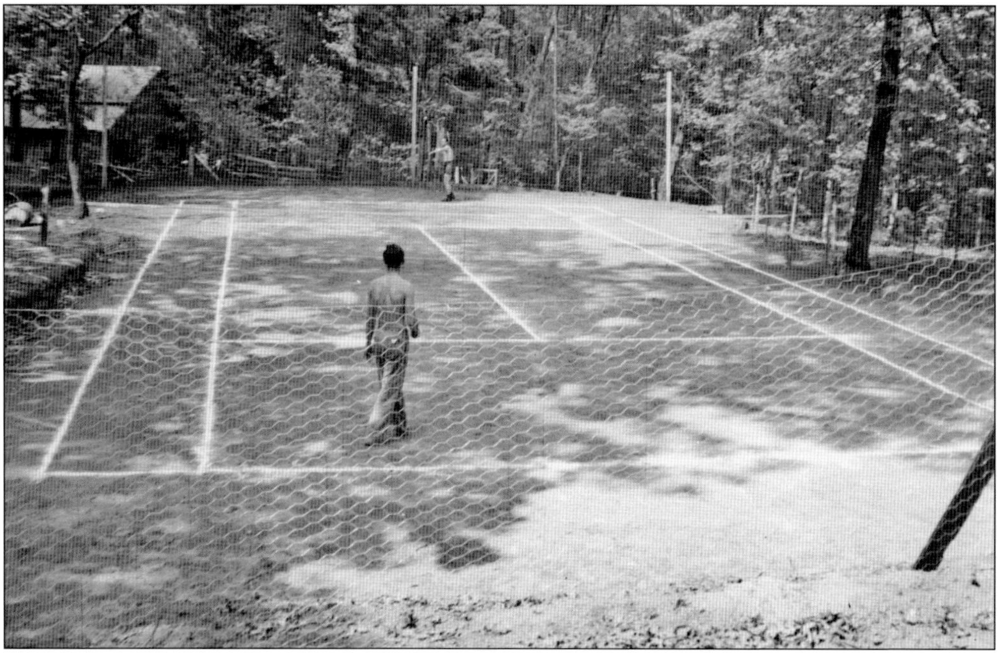

The Hargrove family built a tennis court on the road to the depot and Bobby photographed his friends playing. Although the game of tennis is an old one, the first professional tennis tour of the United States was in 1926. By the 1930s and 1940s, when Bobby took these photographs, home tennis courts were probably rare. Old-time residents of Watkinsville have fond memories of this one. Below, Bobby's friends Rufus Burger (left) and Billy Hodges pose for the camera. Rufus's father was a local judge. Billy Hodges was a pilot.

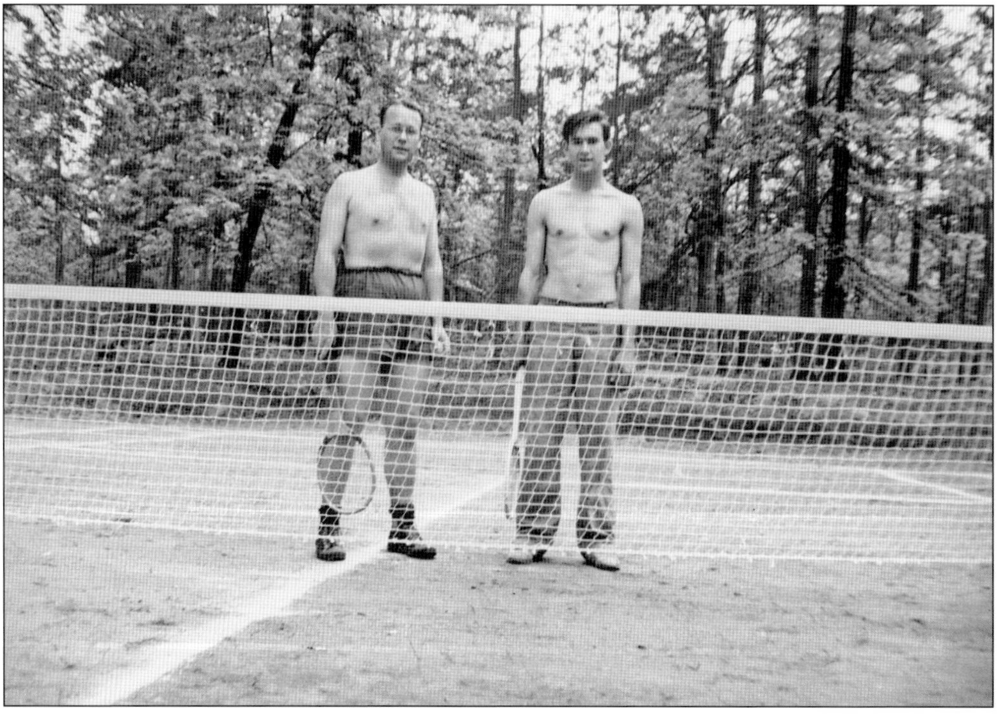

Bobby also took a series of photographs of William Barton Parham lifting weights outside Veale Brothers Hardware store on Main Street. William Parham's father died early, leaving him to support his widowed mother and a sister who had Down syndrome. From 1966 to 1968, Will was the Oconee County tax commissioner. He eventually moved to Florida. The man in the suit watching is C.T. Maxey.

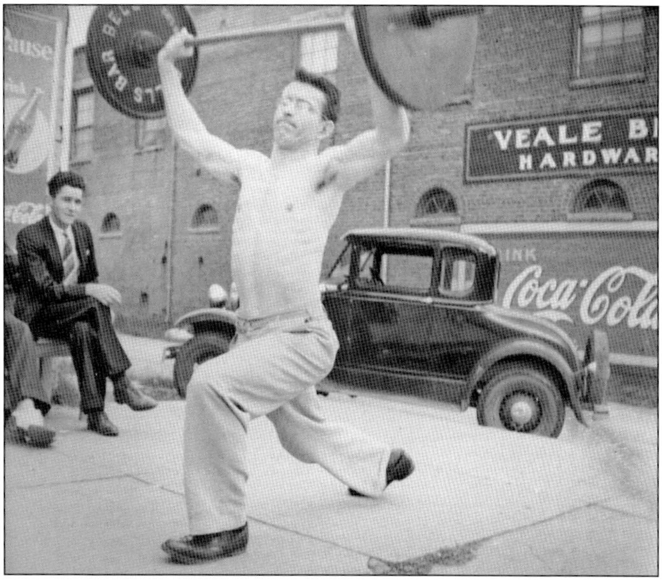

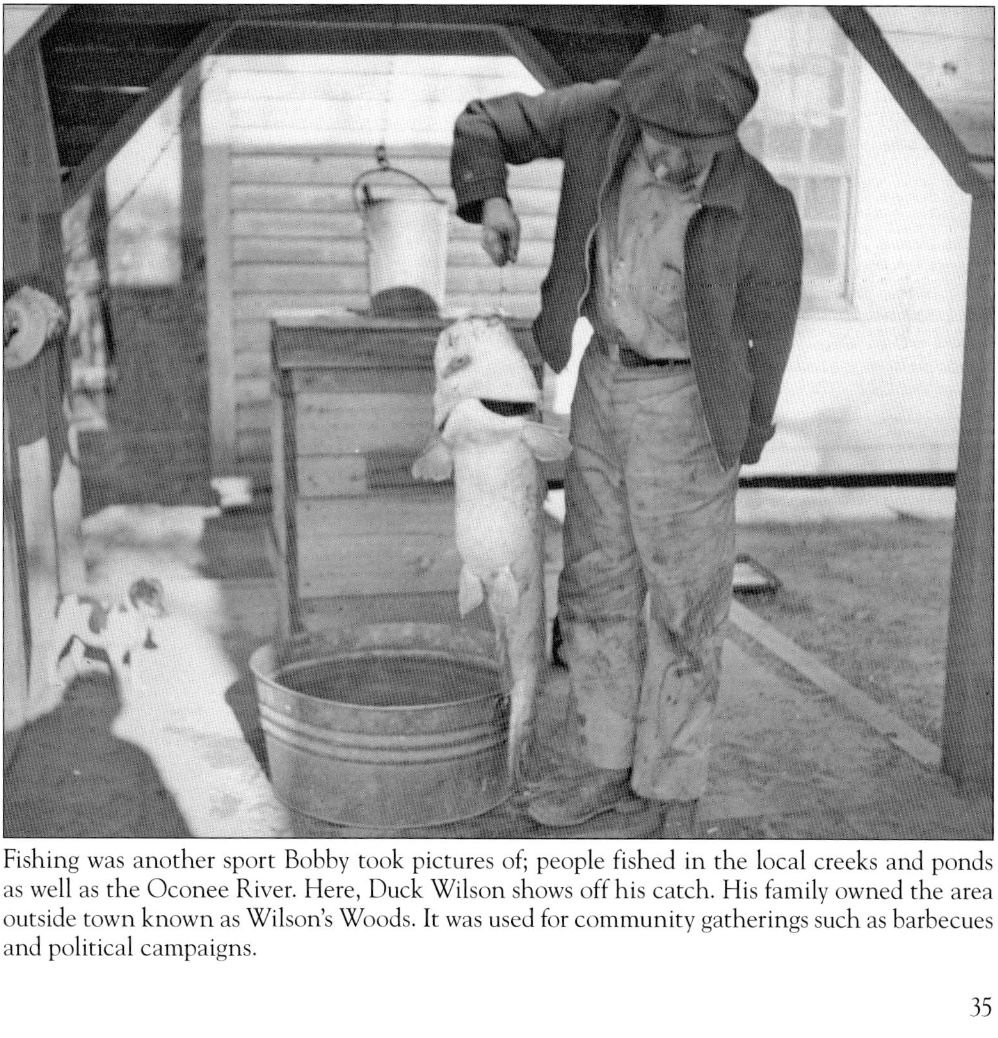

Fishing was another sport Bobby took pictures of; people fished in the local creeks and ponds as well as the Oconee River. Here, Duck Wilson shows off his catch. His family owned the area outside town known as Wilson's Woods. It was used for community gatherings such as barbecues and political campaigns.

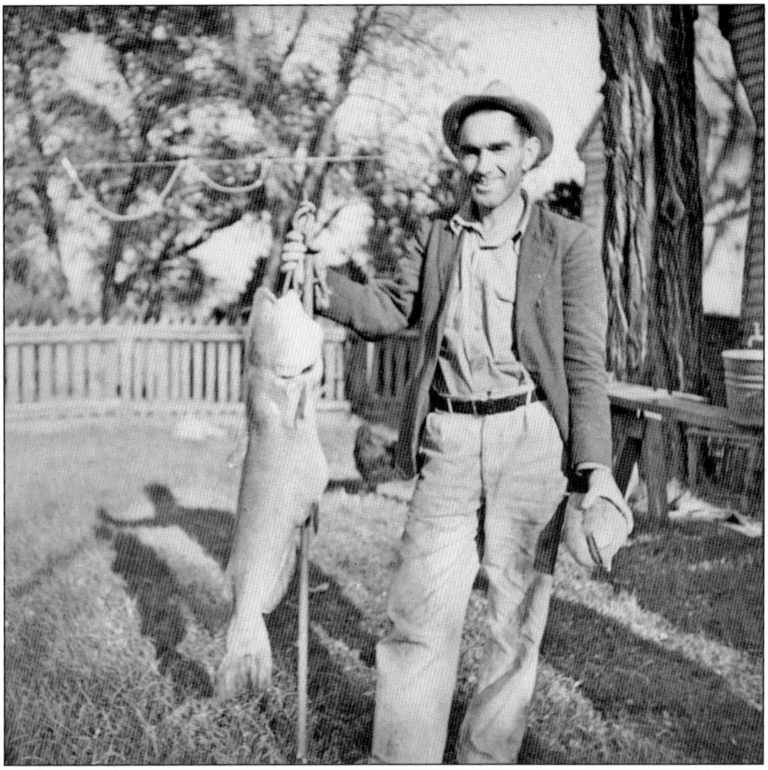

Herbert "Dutch" Hodges is proud of his catch. He ran a store on Main Street that one news article described as the "news center of Watkinsville." One could find out who got on or off the bus or was in jail, all about the 100-pound sturgeon caught at Barnett Shoals, and where the ambulance went. People also gathered around Dutch's Philco radio to listen to Atlanta Cracker baseball games.

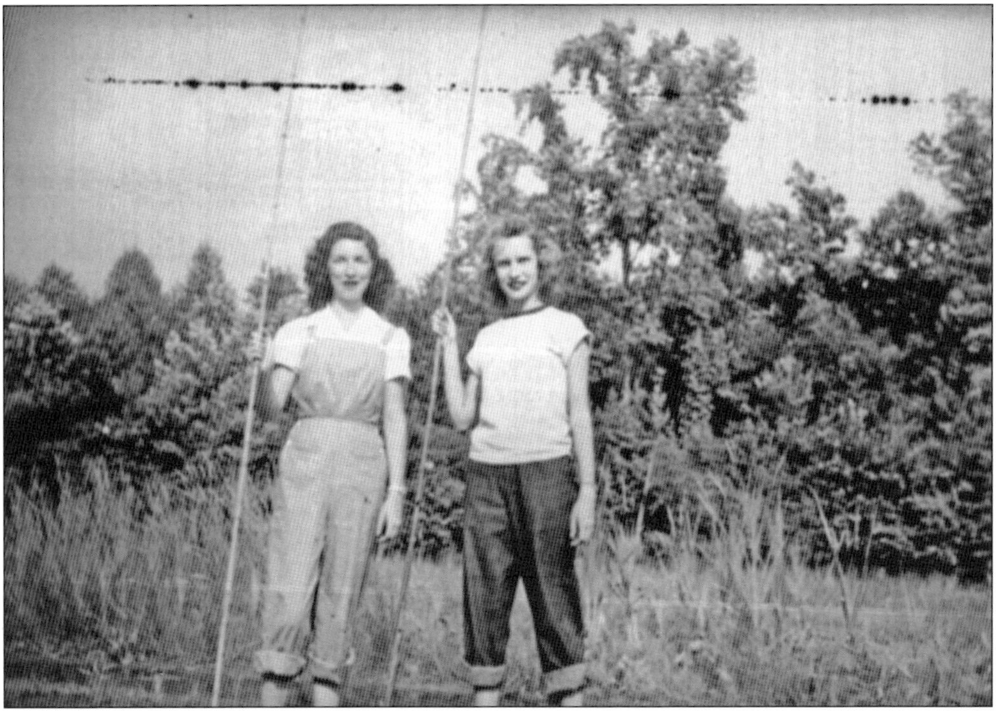

Mary Ashford (left) and Mary Ann Gordon pose with their homemade bamboo fishing rods. Bamboo poles such as these were more common than commercially produced rods.

Four

People around Town

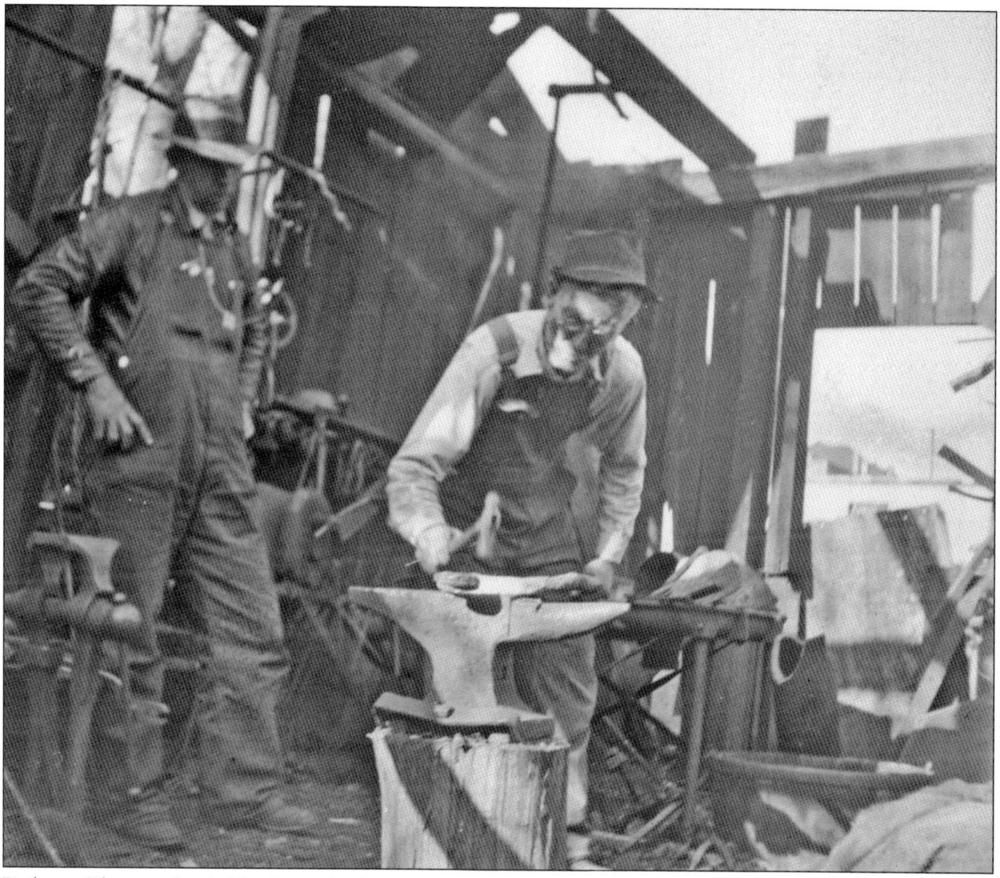

Robert Christopher's blacksmith shop was on Water Street. He had a reputation for being able to repair anything. Roy Ward commented in a 1992 *Oconee Enterprise* article that "Some of us believed he could mend everything but the crack of dawn and a broken heart. . . . He was one of the friendliest men who ever lived and never seemed out of sorts with any person or problem." His shop may look like a shack, but Christopher preferred it that way because it gave him plenty of light to work in.

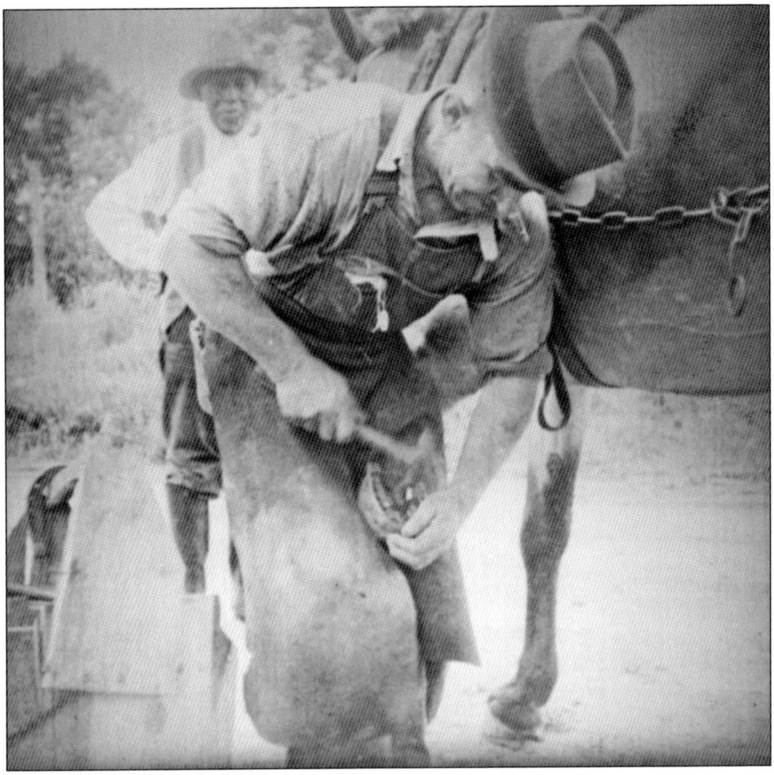

Robert Christopher is shoeing a horse in this photograph. He was especially good at repairing wagon wheels, and also made hoes and other garden tools. He would make smaller rakes for women who needed a shorter one.

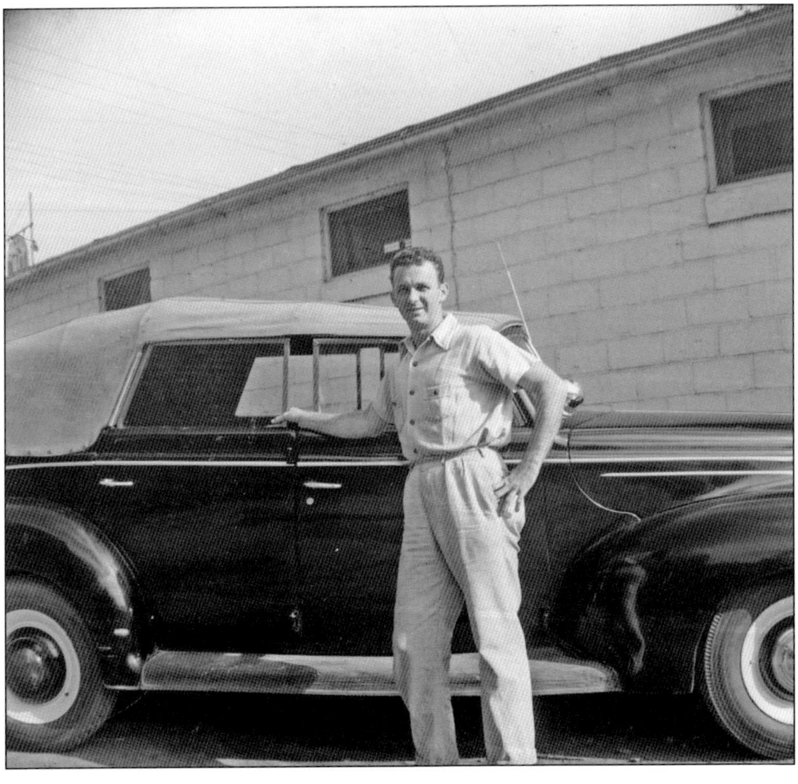

Powell Veale is proudly showing off his Ford convertible. It was probably his first car. He was one of the young men who worked in the Spec Downs store. His nickname was "Tume." He was a member of the Oconee High School class of 1938.

Gatra Osborne married Andrew Jackson. Andrew was the son of Asa M. Jackson, who was the ordinary (probate judge) from 1849 through the 1850s and the original owner of the Fain house. Gatra was a sister of Bobby Gordon's mother. They had a daughter, Charlotte, and eventually moved to Lavonia.

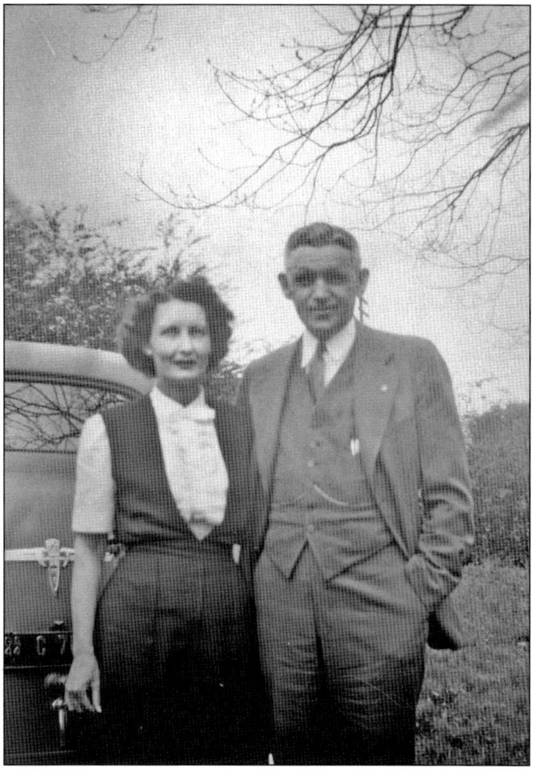

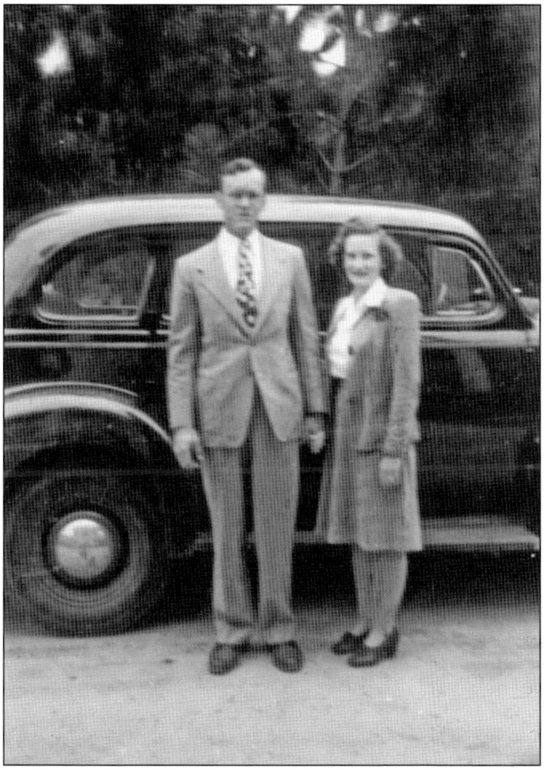

Natalie Rebecca Aiken, a 1939 graduate of Oconee High School, married Arlin O. Wheat. During World War II, the University of Georgia's naval school trained 2,000 combat pilots. Wheat taught them preflight training. The Wheats remained in the area, as Natalie was listed as part of the committee that organized the 50th reunion for the Oconee County High School Alumni Society in 1989.

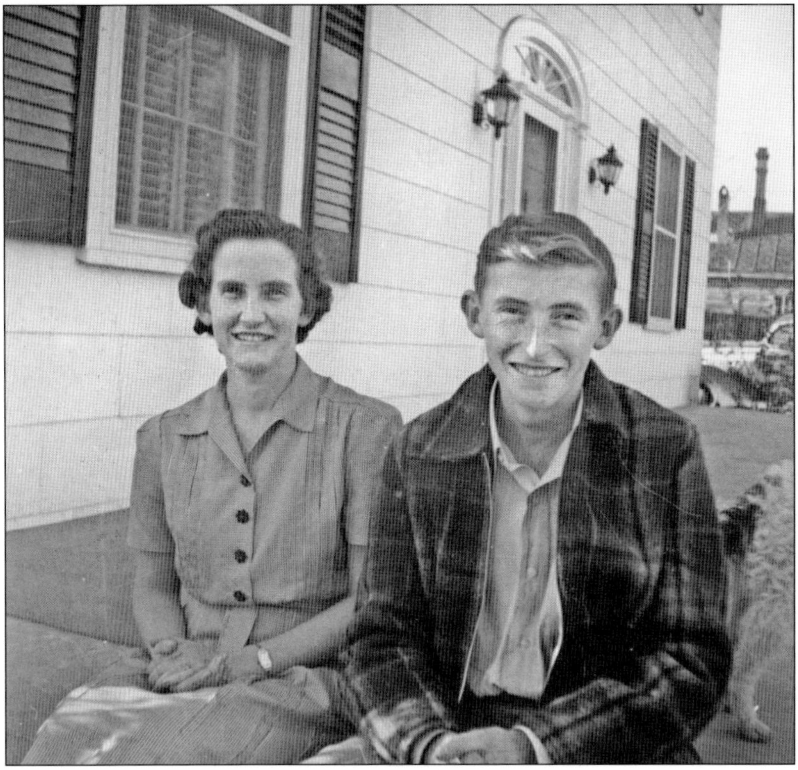

Natalie Aiken Wheat was Nathan Aiken's daughter. She is pictured with her brother Billy.

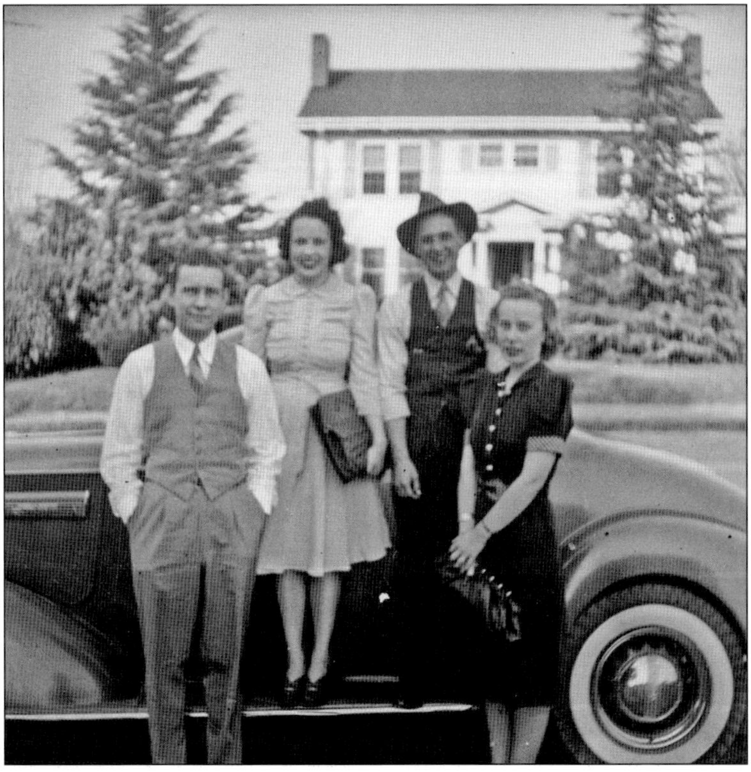

The people in this photograph are, from left to right, Charles Gordon, Mildred Osborne, unidentified, and Vivian Ward. Vivian was raised on a farm on the Old Greensboro Road. She was a quiet, unassuming, but plain-spoken woman who loved the land, animals, nature, and the environment. Her will created the David Hardigree Wildlife Sanctuary, named after her grandfather, so that the farm would remain forever as a home for wildlife and an educational center.

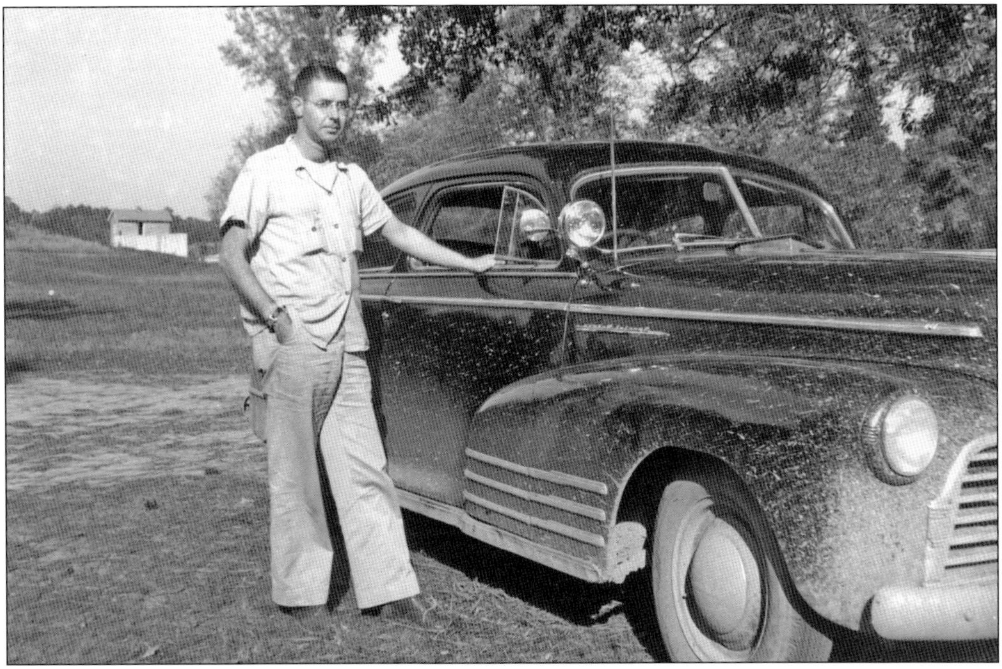

After he returned from World War II, Bill Whitehead became a rural mail carrier from 1947 to 1973. His father, William Walker Whitehead, was the first rural mail carrier hired in Watkinsville in 1903; his route carried him into the countryside, where roads were narrow and pavement was unheard of. He depended on his horse Jacket to carry his mail wagon from place to place. He created a sensation when he switched to a car.

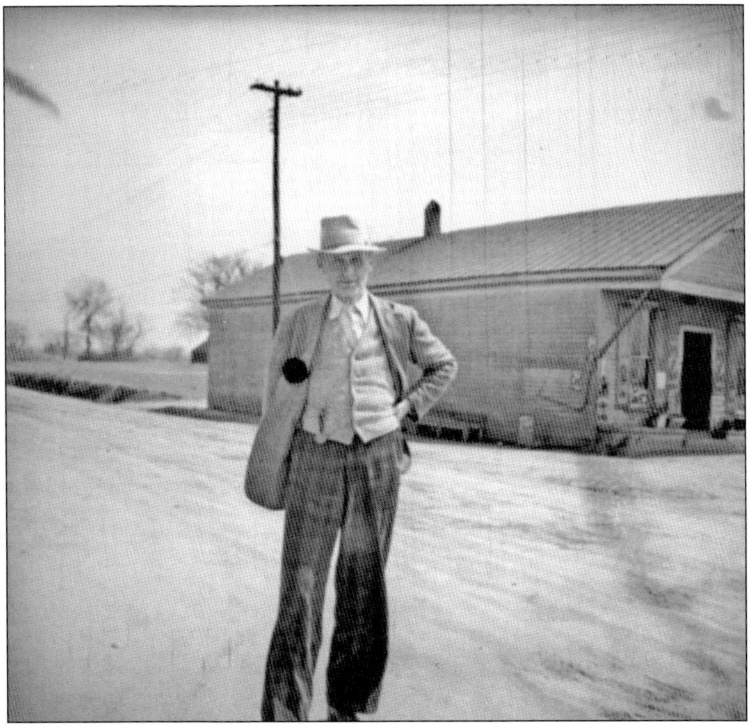

Diamond Veale worked as an undertaker. He also owned Veale's Hardware Store on Main Street. The building behind him is the McRee & Co. store, which was located on the south corner of what is now Barnett Shoals Road and Highway 15.

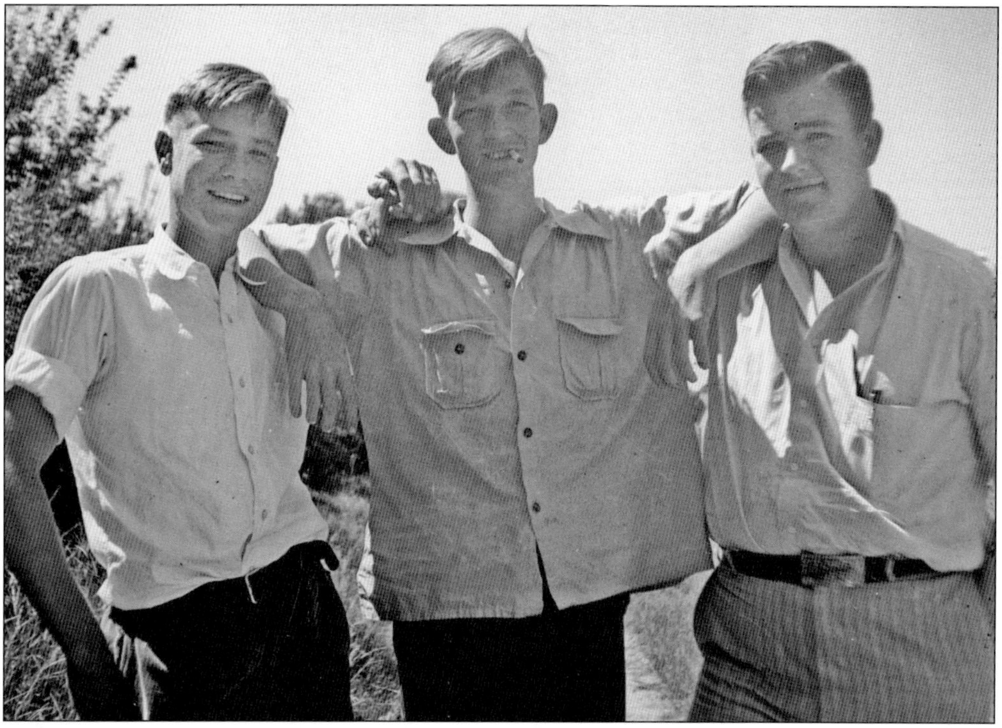

These three young men are, from left to right, Langford Hodges, Irvin "Tadpole" McGuire, and Jack Barnett.

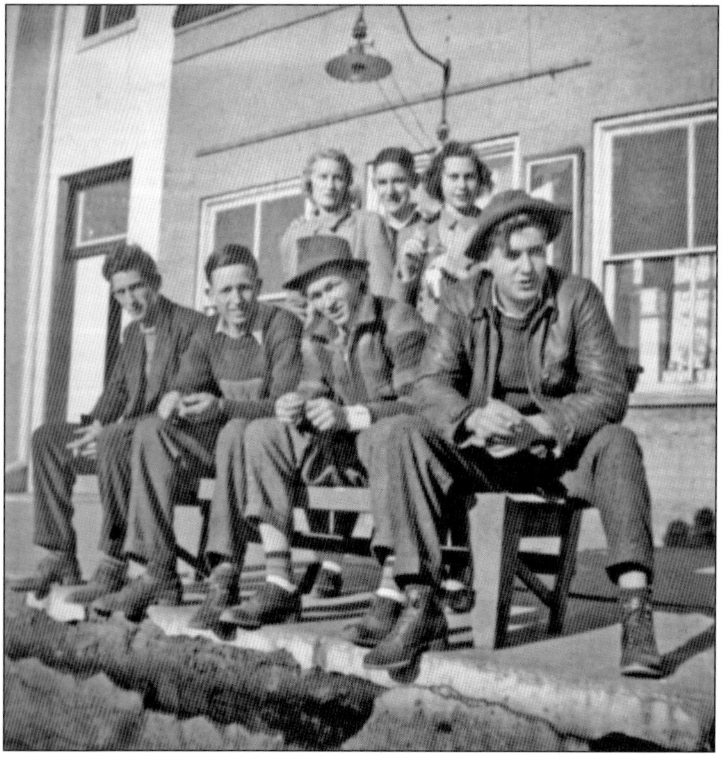

The people posing on one of the many benches along Main Street are, from left to right, (first row) Bruce Anderson, Henry Vernon, Irvin McGuire, and Asa Whitehead; (second row) Anita Chandler, Langford Hodges, and Joan Camp. Henry Vernon lived on a farm on the other side of the Watkinsville Cemetery.

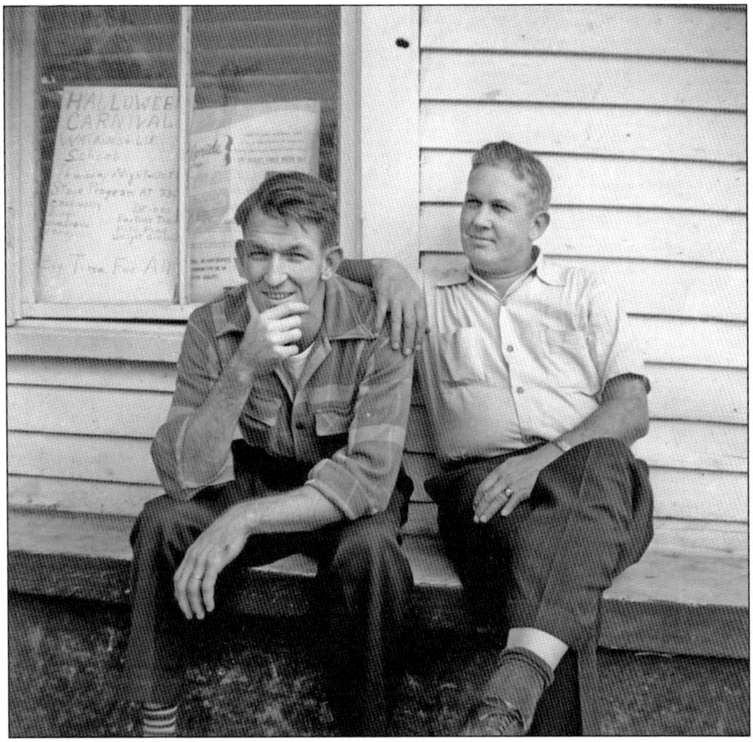

These two men are Irvin McGuire (left) and Harry McDonald. Irvin was decorated in World War II. Harry was a member of the Oconee High School class of 1940. Notice the Halloween Carnival sign in the window. Activities included a stage program, cake walking, bingo, sideshows, candy, drinks, fortune telling, a fish pond, weight guessing, and a "Big Time For All." The other poster is advertising motor oil.

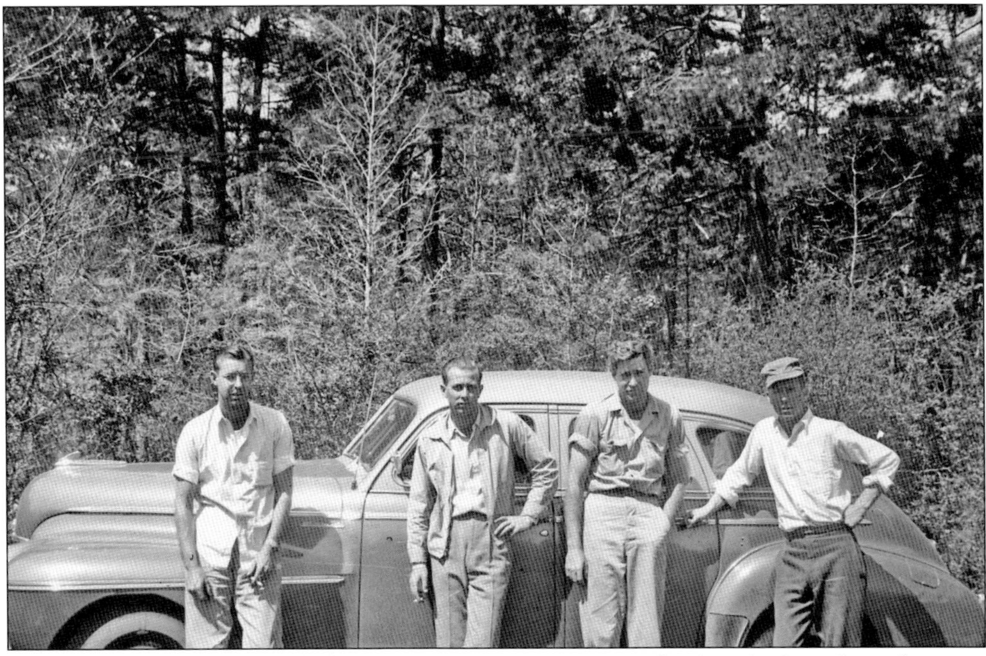

When World War II started, these young men were among the first draftees from the area. From left to right are William "Bill" Whitehead, Gerald McRee, Asa Whitehead, and Francis "Doot" Smith. Gerald was one of the young men who ran the Spec Downs store. Doot married a schoolteacher. Bill and Asa were brothers. All four became charter members of the Veterans of Foreign Wars Post 9147, organized in 1947.

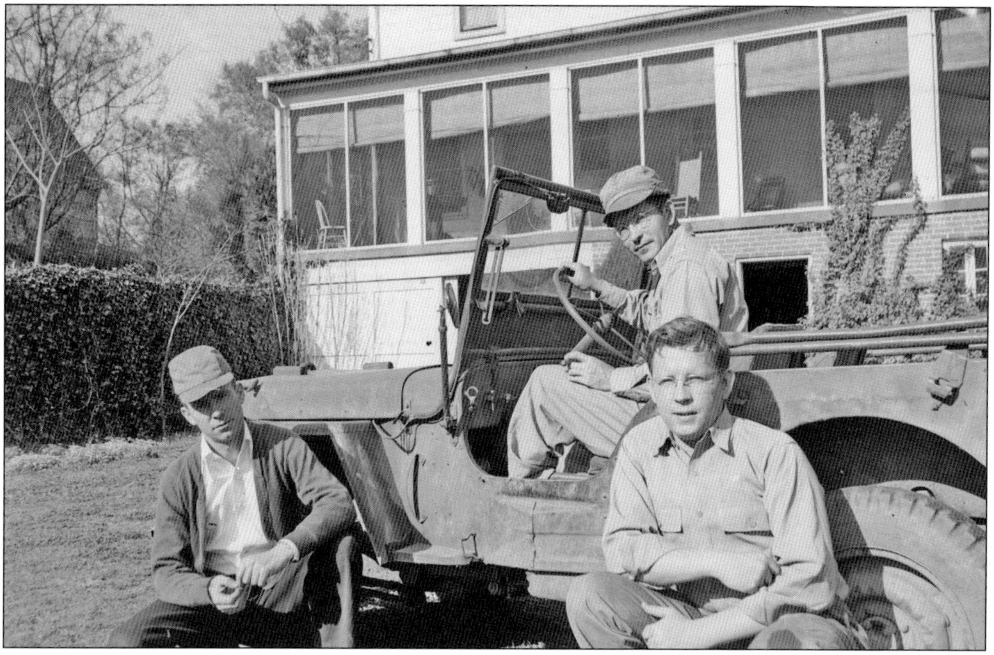

From left to right, Doot Smith, "Cootie" Parham, and Bobby Gordon are posing with a jeep in the backyard of the Fain house. Nicknames such as those mentioned here and elsewhere in this book were common in this period.

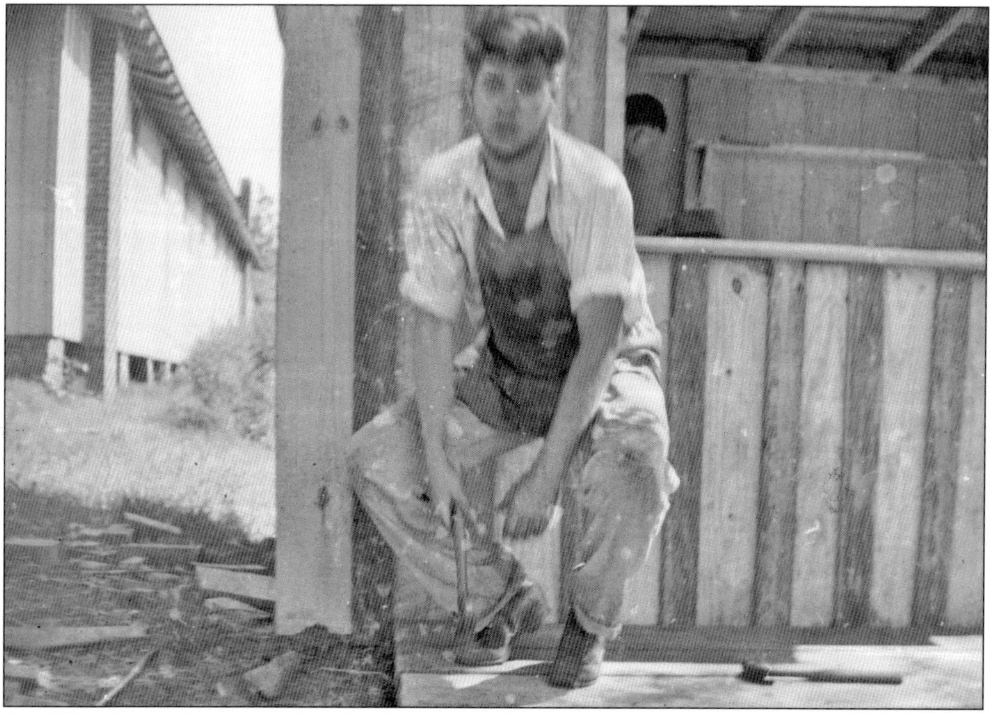

Asa Whitehead, Oconee High School class of 1938, never married and lived with his sister Louisa in the old family homestead off New High Shoals Road. He worked for Dairy Pak in Athens. The building he is working on is a concession stand. The gym is the building to the left.

Oswald Billups's nickname was "Mudcat." He was a cheerful companion to everyone from children to the elderly. One favorite memory of some of the men still around today is of the cave they dug. They also dammed a creek. Oswald was one of the diggers. He was in the Navy during World War II. Afterwards, he took over his father's drugstore. He eventually moved to Toccoa, where he worked for Le Tourneau Industries.

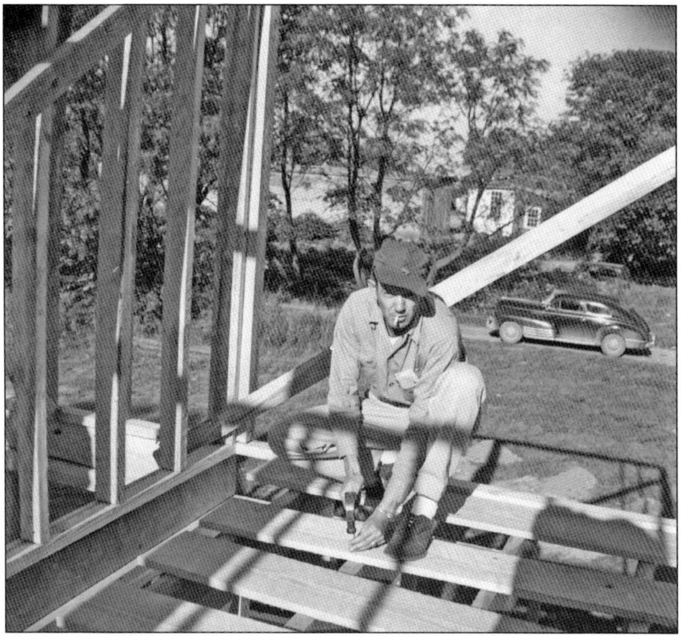

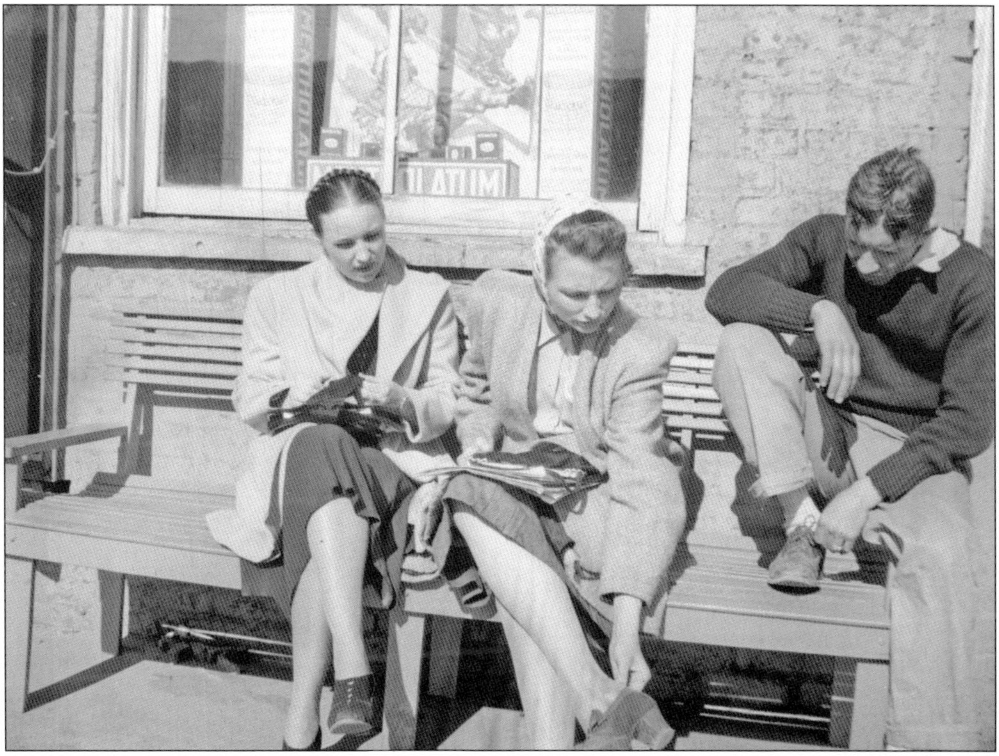

From left to right, Louisa Whitehead, Florine Stovall, and Oswald Billups gather on Main Street. Louisa and Flo became teachers. Louisa taught fifth grade and high school English and Latin. She eventually became the principal of Bishop Elementary and of schools in Athens. Flo was a first-grade teacher in Watkinsville and Athens known for her patience, great sense of humor, and a magical sense of empathy and rapport that endeared her to her students.

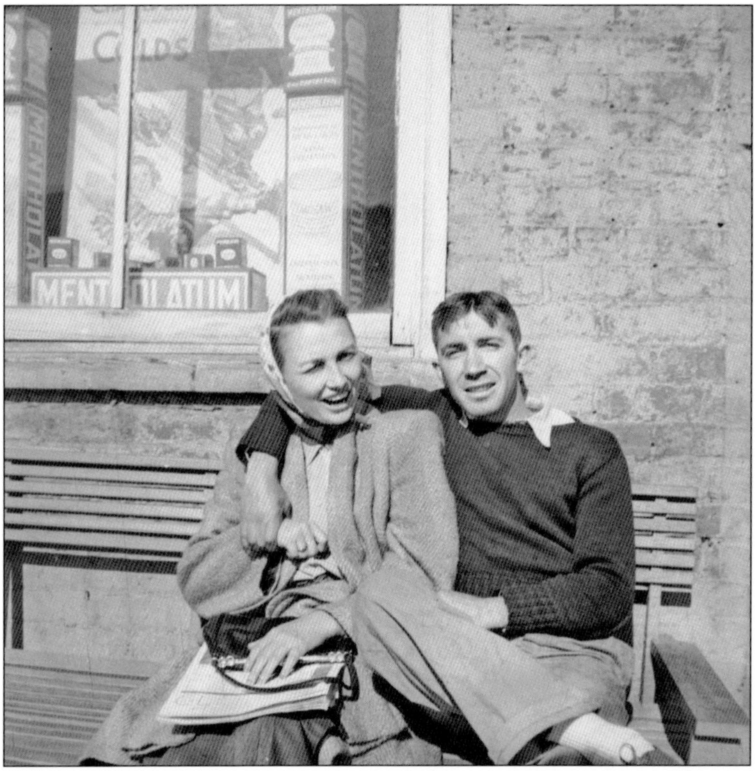

Flo Stovall was a member of the first Girl Scout troop in Oconee County (founded in 1914). She remembers camping at Snows Mill. Each girl got to cook over her own fire. The leaders brought guitars so they could sing around the campfire, and Walter Downs (the brother of Katie Downs, the leader), would tell a story that would last the whole week they were camping. Stovall is pictured with Oswald Billups.

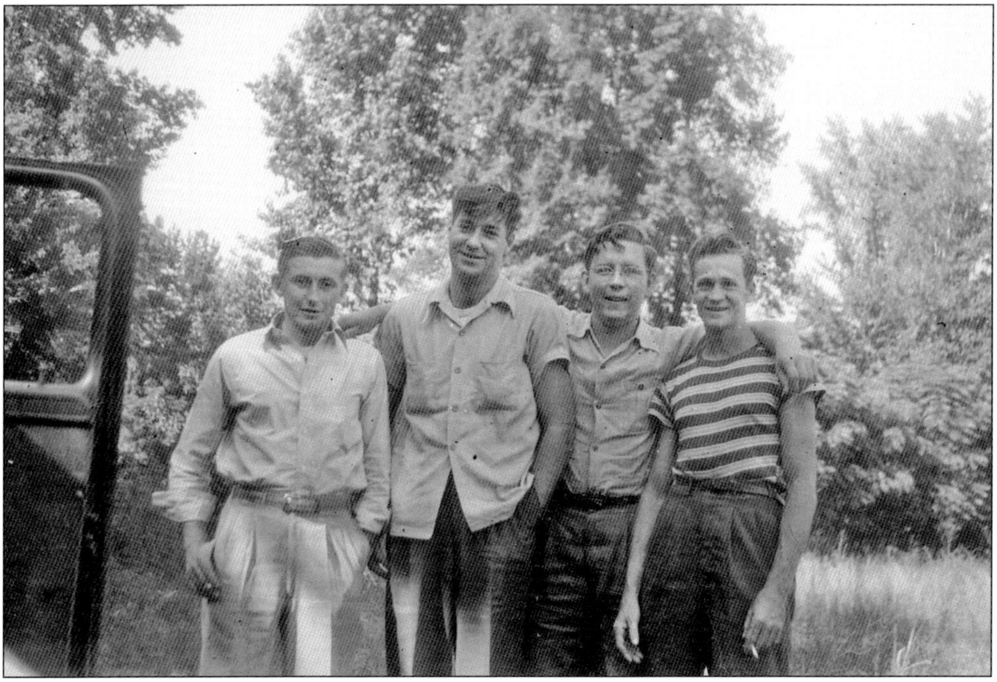

The young men in this photograph are, from left to right, friends Billy Aiken, Asa Whitehead, Bobby Gordon, and Gerald McRee. Bobby frequently used a tripod and timer to take photographs like this one. After he posed his subjects, he would run to get into the picture.

Gerald McRee worked at the Spec Downs store. He had a wry sense of humor and an instant wit that, along with his obvious love for others, endeared him to his customers. During World War II, he served in the South Pacific with the 5th and 13th Army Air Corps. He became Watkinsville's acting postmaster in 1960 and the postmaster in 1962. He moved to Daytona, Florida, after he retired.

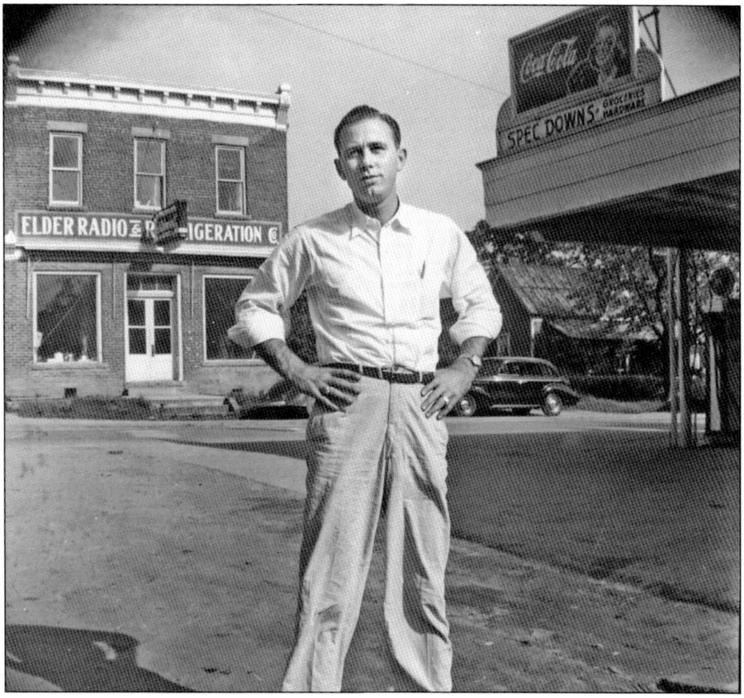

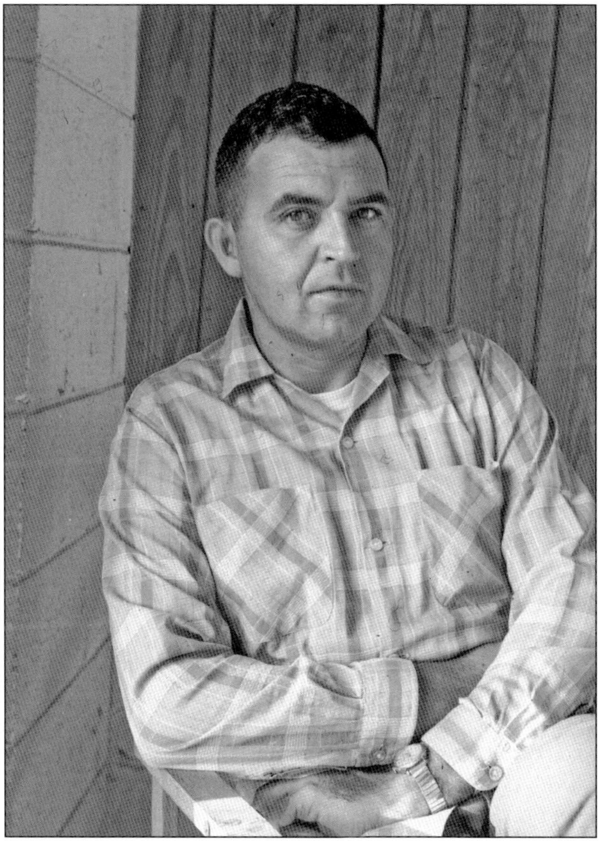

Billy Dawson taught school. The Monroe High School class of 1965 said Bill was quick to discern who had a talent for writing. He nurtured them, "prodding and pushing us along hoping to make us see the potential locked deep inside ourselves. He could read a passage of literature with all the softness and tenderness of angel wings or scare the beegeezus out of us with his lion-like roar."

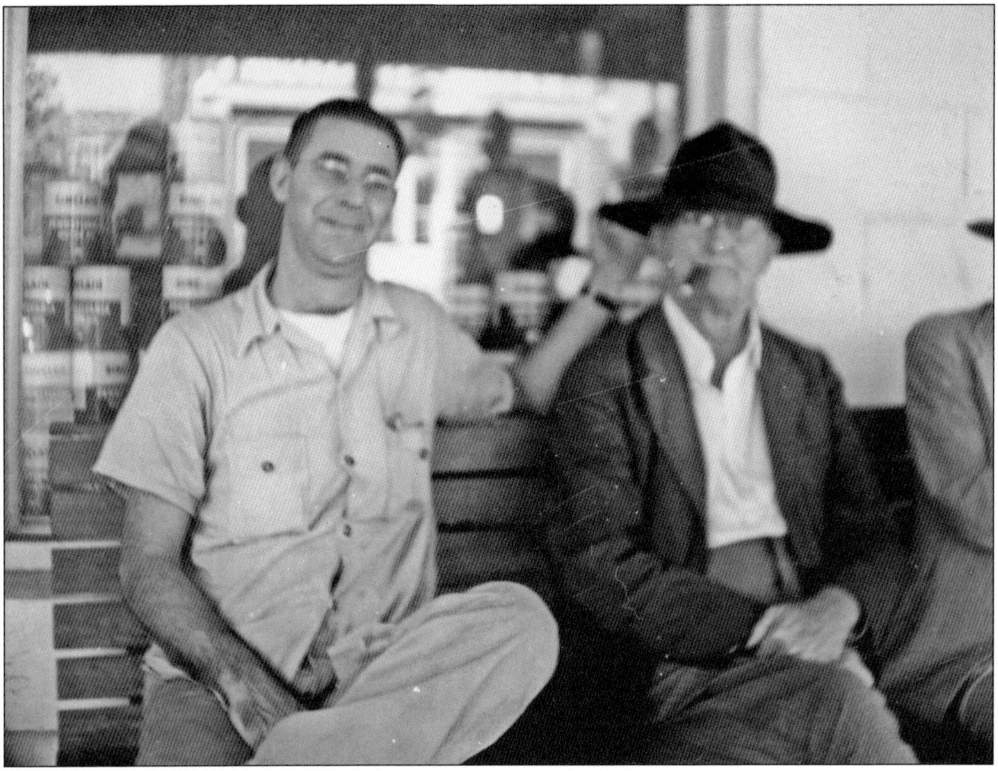

William Whitehead (left) and Henry Burgess pose for Bobby's camera. Henry lived on Main Street. During the 1930s and 1940s, when many people did not own cars, they would gather on the benches outside the stores to wait for someone with a car willing to drive them into Athens. Buses also ran between Watkinsville and Athens and stopped along Main Street.

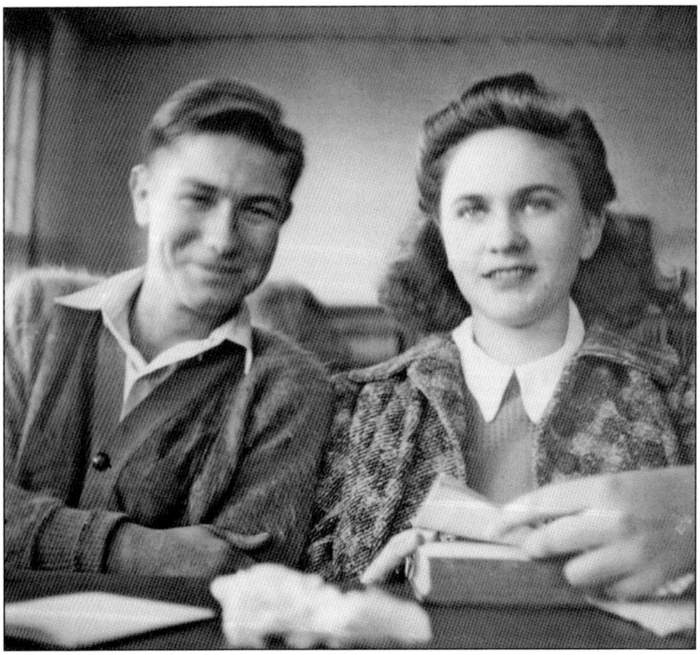

Chase Bishop graduated in 1940 from Oconee High School, where he played basketball. He also had a beautiful singing voice. Elma Anthony was the daughter of the school superintendent, Elmer N. Anthony. She married Irvin McGuire and worked for the Social Security Administration.

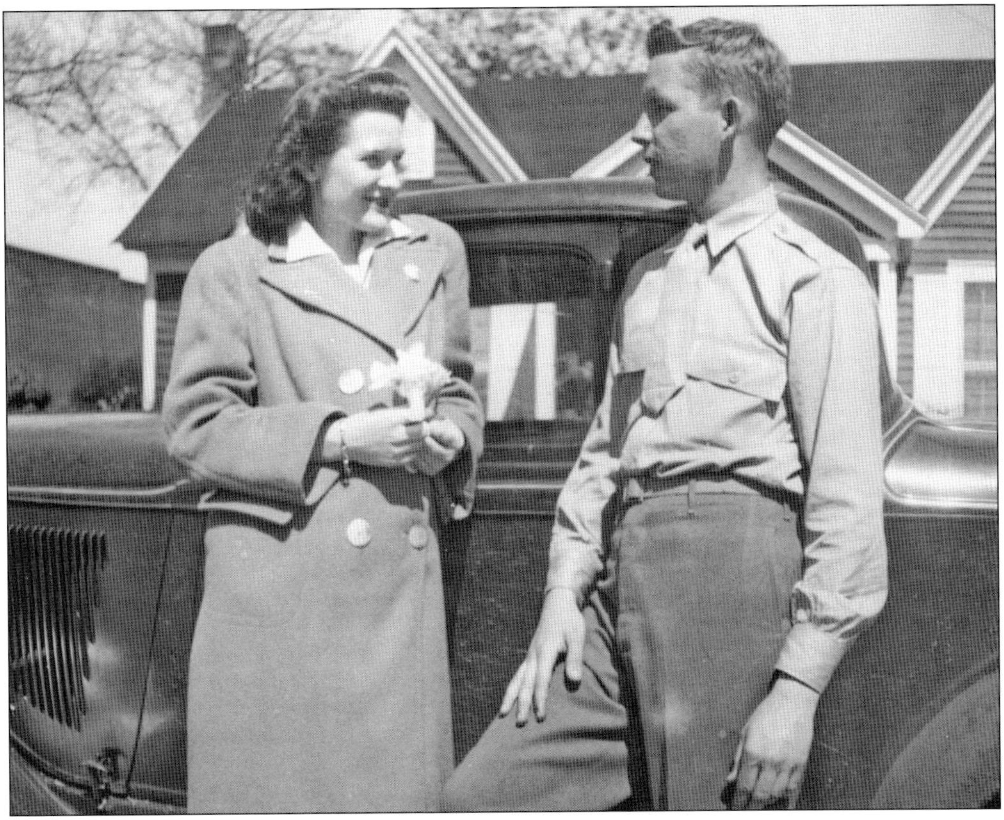

This photograph of Elma Anthony and Bobby Gordon was taken on Main Street in front of the old Gordon home.

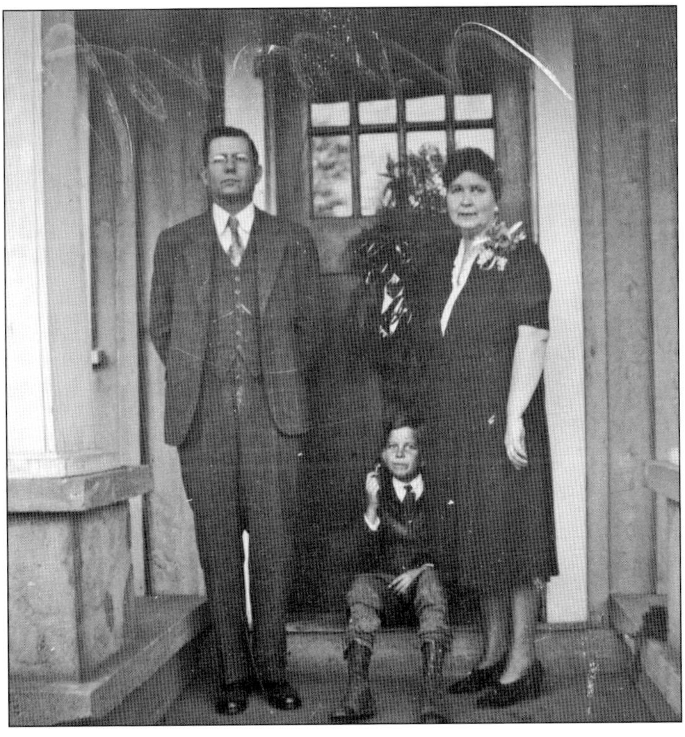

Burney Hale was the county's tax receiver (now tax commissioner) from 1933 to 1943. He became Watkinsville's acting postmaster in 1947 and was promoted to postmaster in 1949. His wife is Lucy Elder Hale. The young man is their son Bob Hale. Bob earned a Bronze Star in the Korean War.

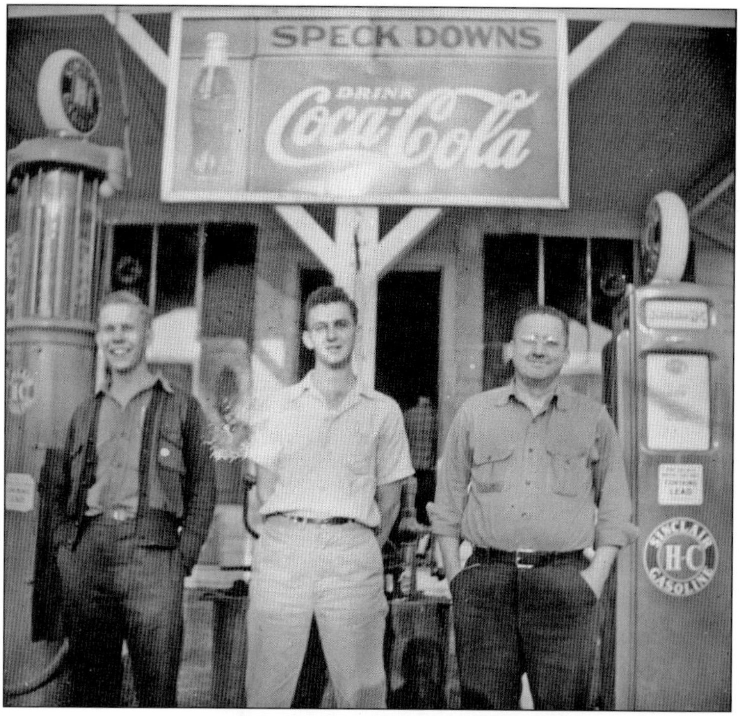

The Spec Downs store, located on the north side of Barnett Shoals Road, was one of the busiest. He took telephone orders, which were quickly delivered. He sold local products such as Mr. Dempsey's honey, Dorris Marshall's sausage, and Mrs. Ward's chocolate milk and homegrown vegetables. Spec and his wife, Harriet, considered the young men who worked for him "Spec's boys." Pictured from left to right are Norris Gordon, Powell Veale, and Spec Downs.

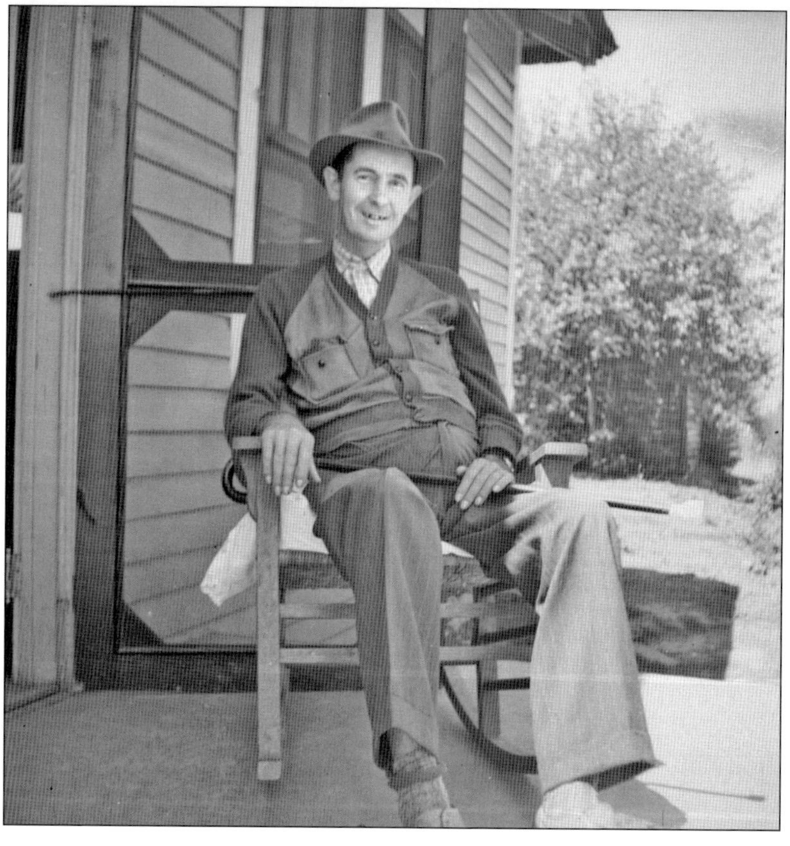

Herman O'Dillon was elected clerk of the superior court in 1936. Robert Ashford described him as "one of the best and most efficient officials that the county has ever had." He also had the ability to make friends and to see the humorous side of life.

Grady Wheeler won a statewide speech contest. He was a member of the Oconee High School class of 1940.

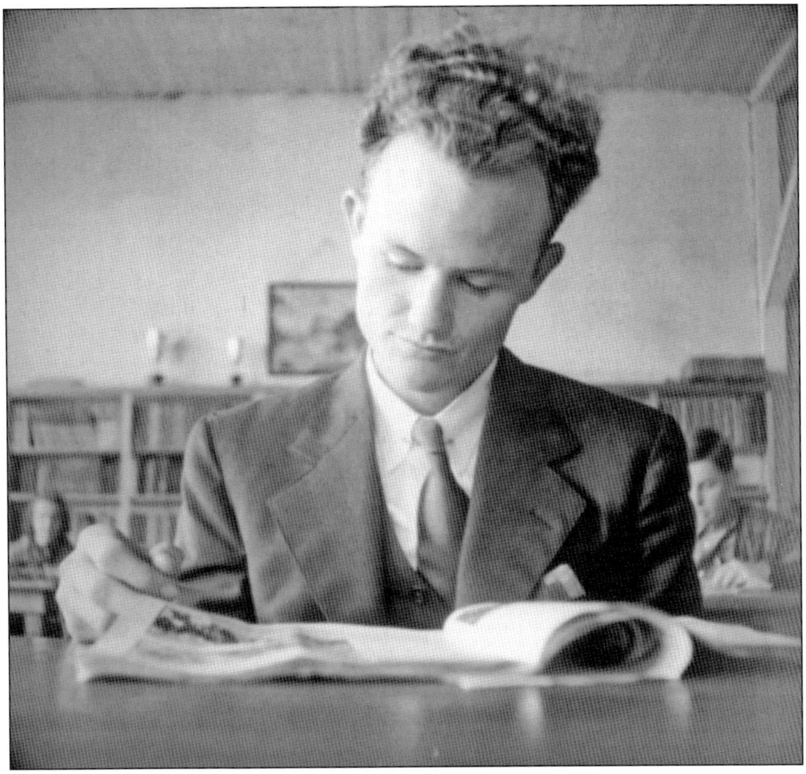

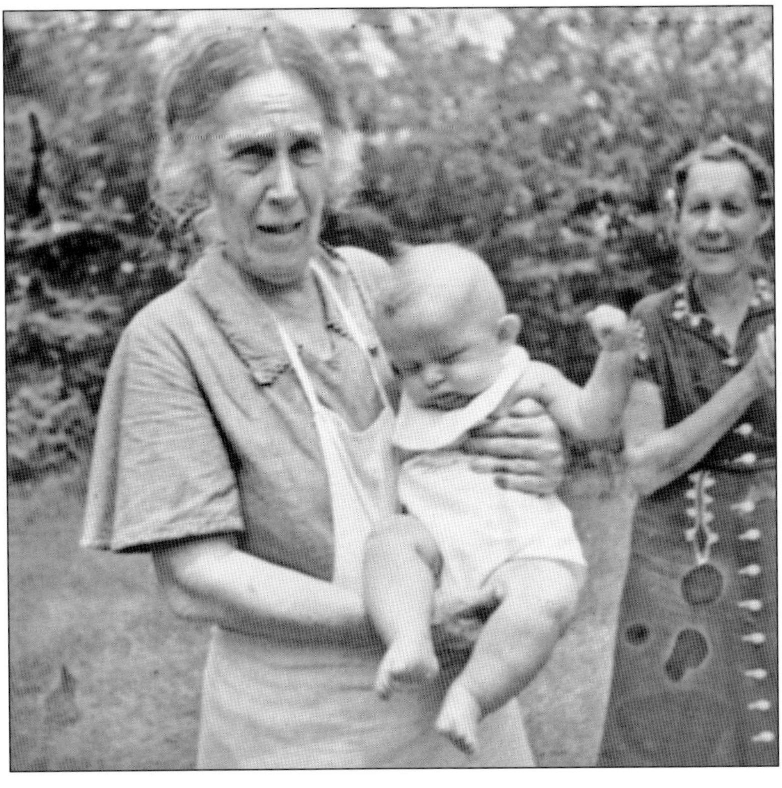

The woman with the unidentified baby is Ida Murray. Behind her is Mary Gordon. Ida was a milliner in Athens. She was considered eccentric because, at a time when women did not do such things, she did much of the work of building her house on Main Street, including hauling bricks in a wheelbarrow from the railroad yard. She died at the age of 92 in 1952.

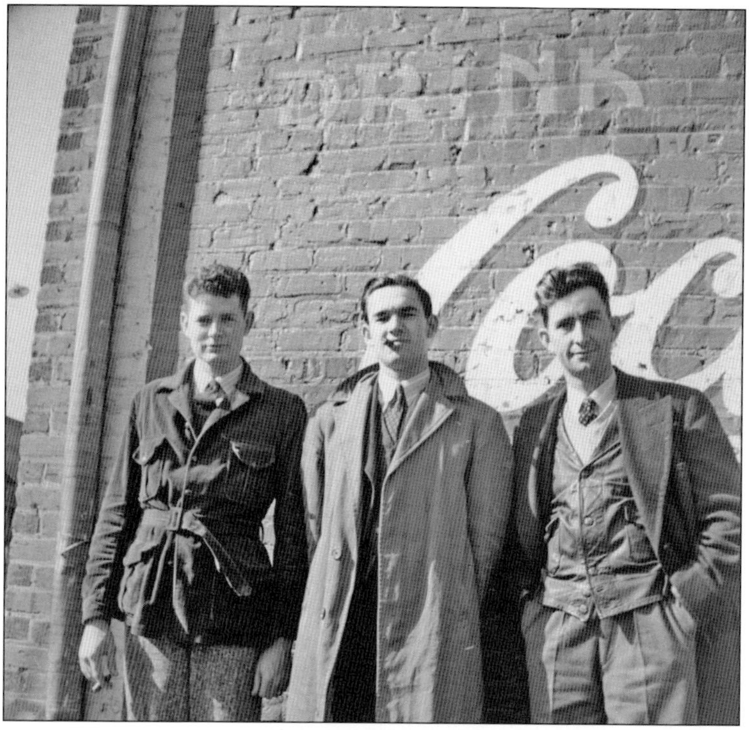

From left to right, Mayne Elder, Billy Hodges, and an unidentified man stand in front of one of the many "Drink Coca Cola" signs around town. Mayne eventually worked in Washington, DC, as the chief of staff for a congressman.

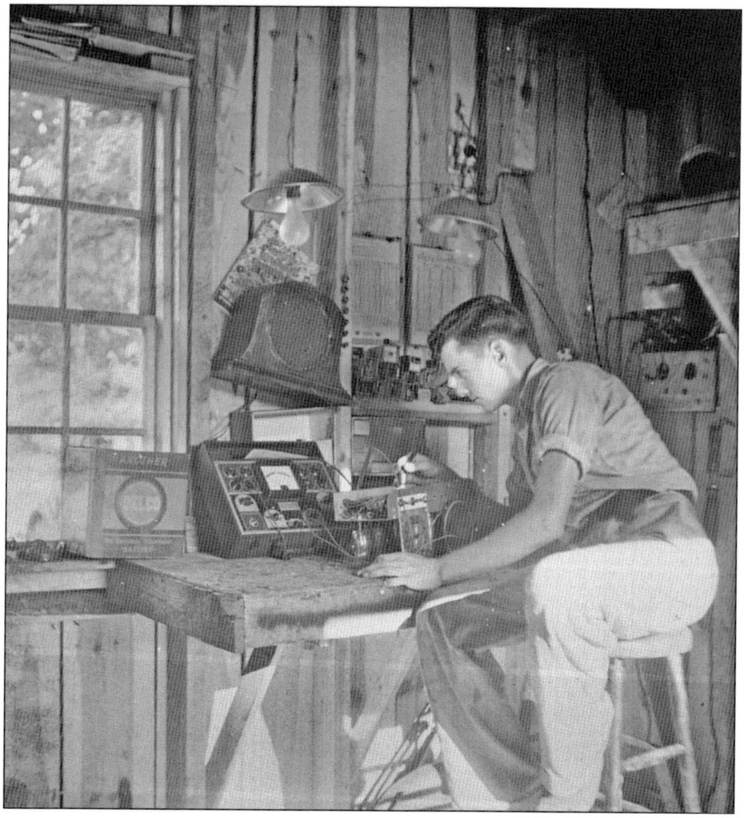

The radio this unidentified young man is working on is stripped of its outer cover and is upside down on the bench in front of him. A closer look shows the vacuum tubes, which often needed repair. He is holding a test probe in his right hand that he is probably using to check components of the radio for functionality. On the wall is a 1920s remote speaker. The nearby shelf holds other test equipment.

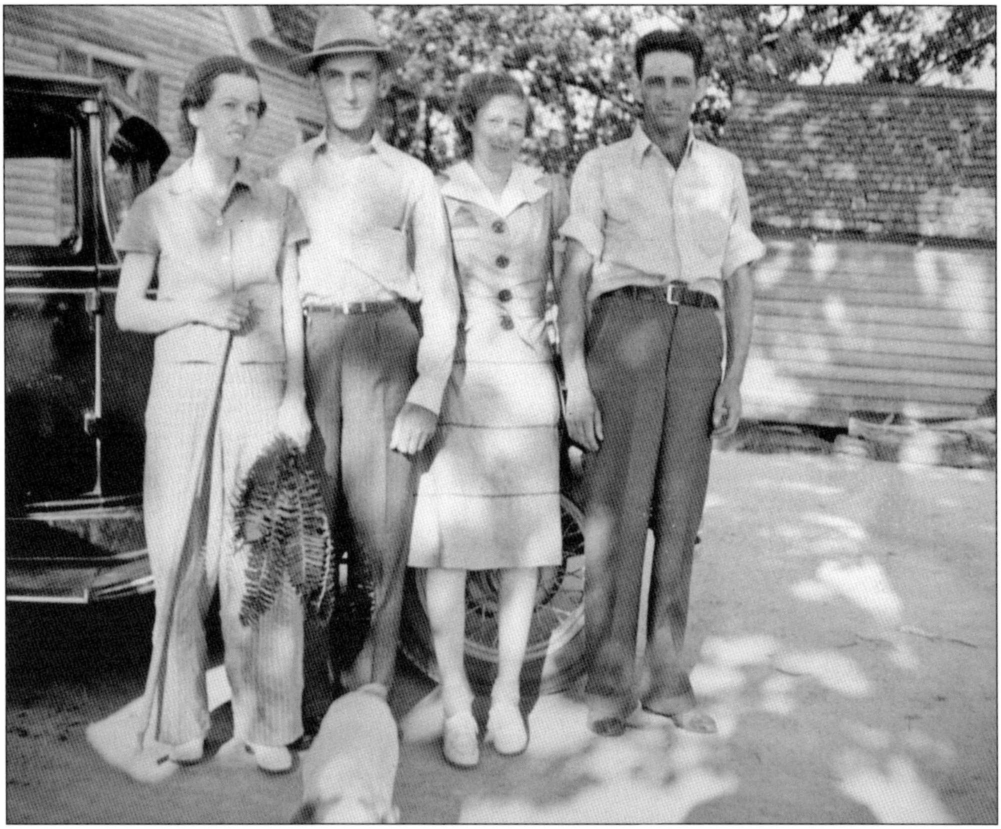

Sarah Edna Bell and her husband, Julian Aiken (the couple on the left), are posing with an unidentified couple in this photograph.

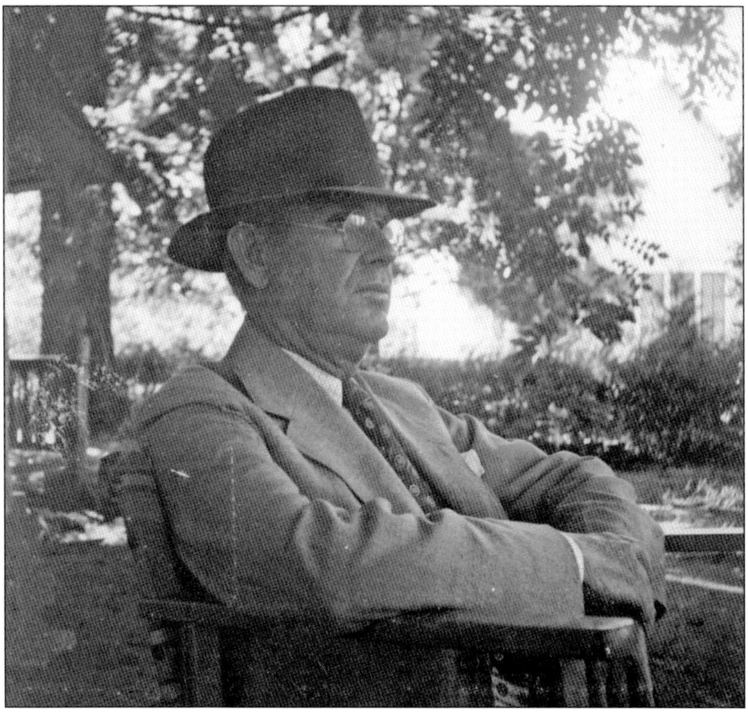

Robert Ashford's father, A.W., set up a gas station on Main Street for him to run, but his favorite activity was writing poetry. He also wrote *Historical Sketches and Reminiscences of Georgia*, a book of sketches of famous Georgians, some local men, and towns.

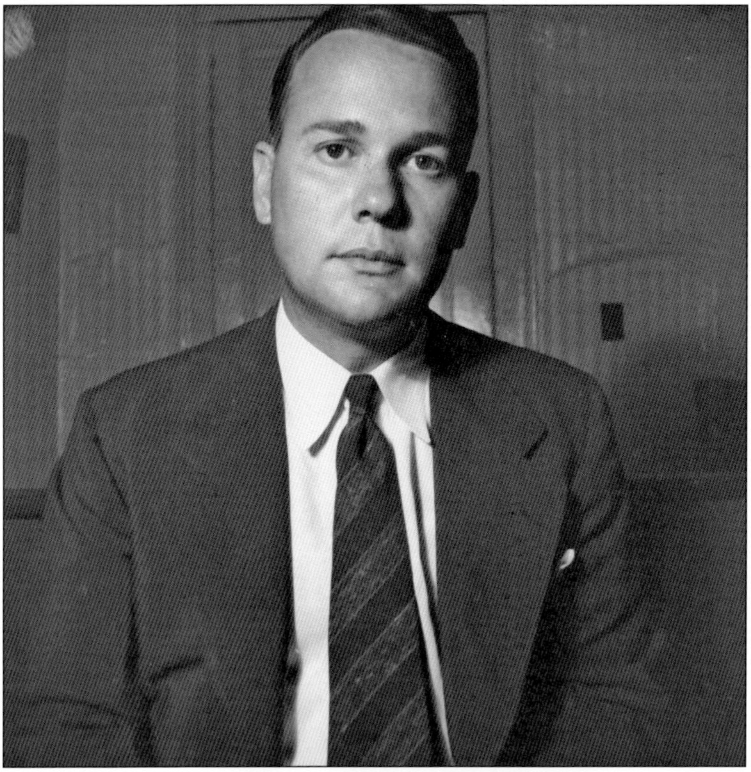

Rufus Burger became a school teacher. Students of Bogart High School remember him as a basketball coach. He eventually taught math at Atlanta High School. His family lived in the first house across the railroad tracks from South Main Street on Colham Ferry Road.

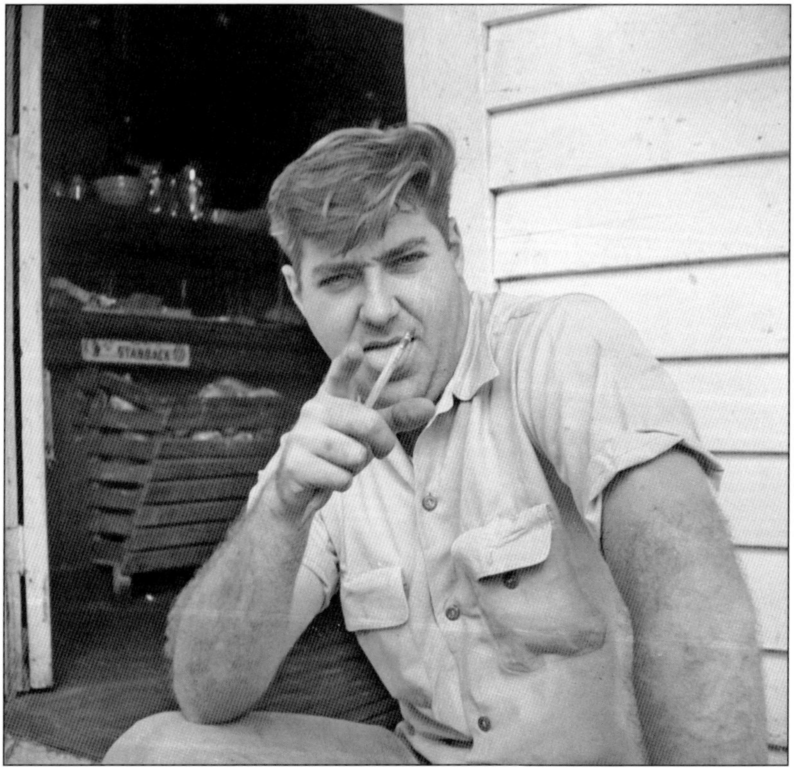

Asa Whitehead was captured on film taking a break on the porch of one of the grocery stores in Watkinsville by Bobby. The bin behind him appears to be full of potatoes.

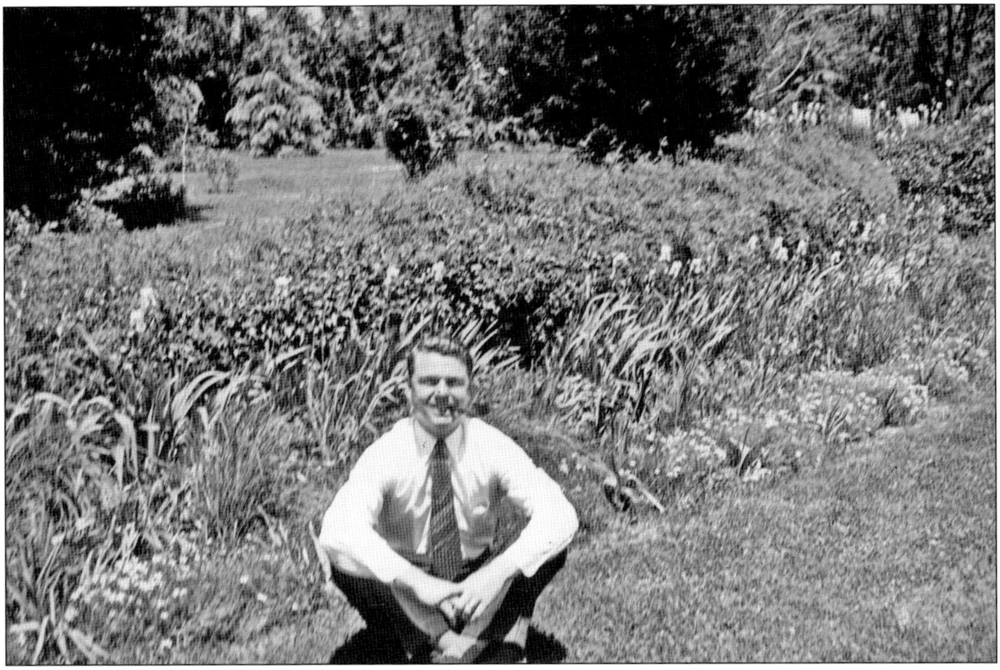

Martha Fain, Bobby's aunt, was well known for her garden. Billy Hodges may be sitting in front of her flowers.

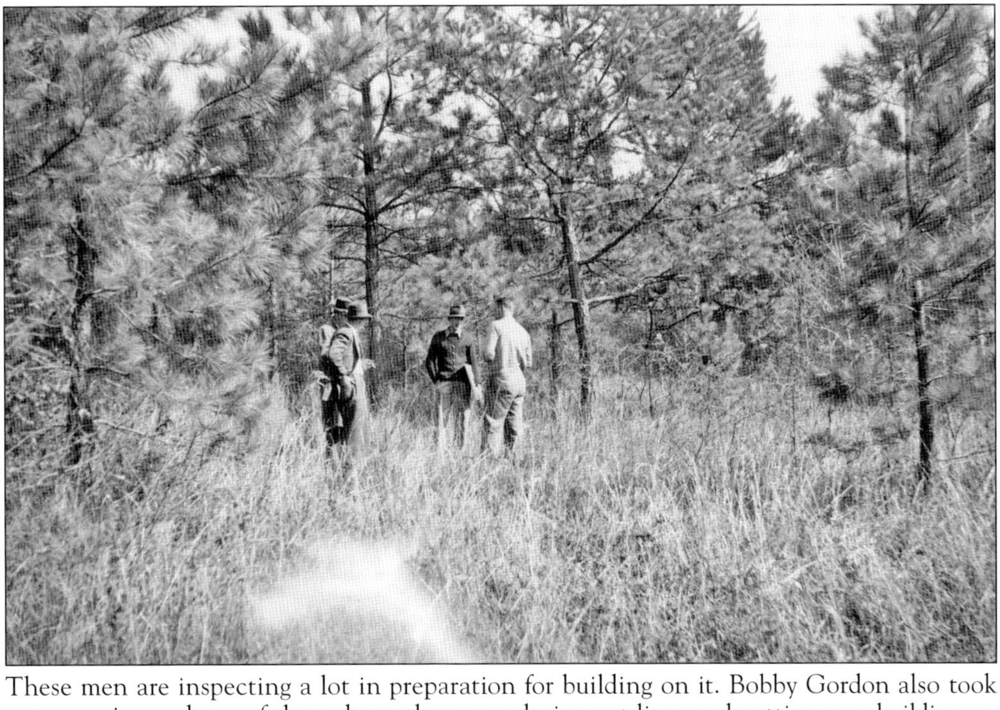

These men are inspecting a lot in preparation for building on it. Bobby Gordon also took some movies, and one of them shows these men laying out lines and putting up a building on this lot.

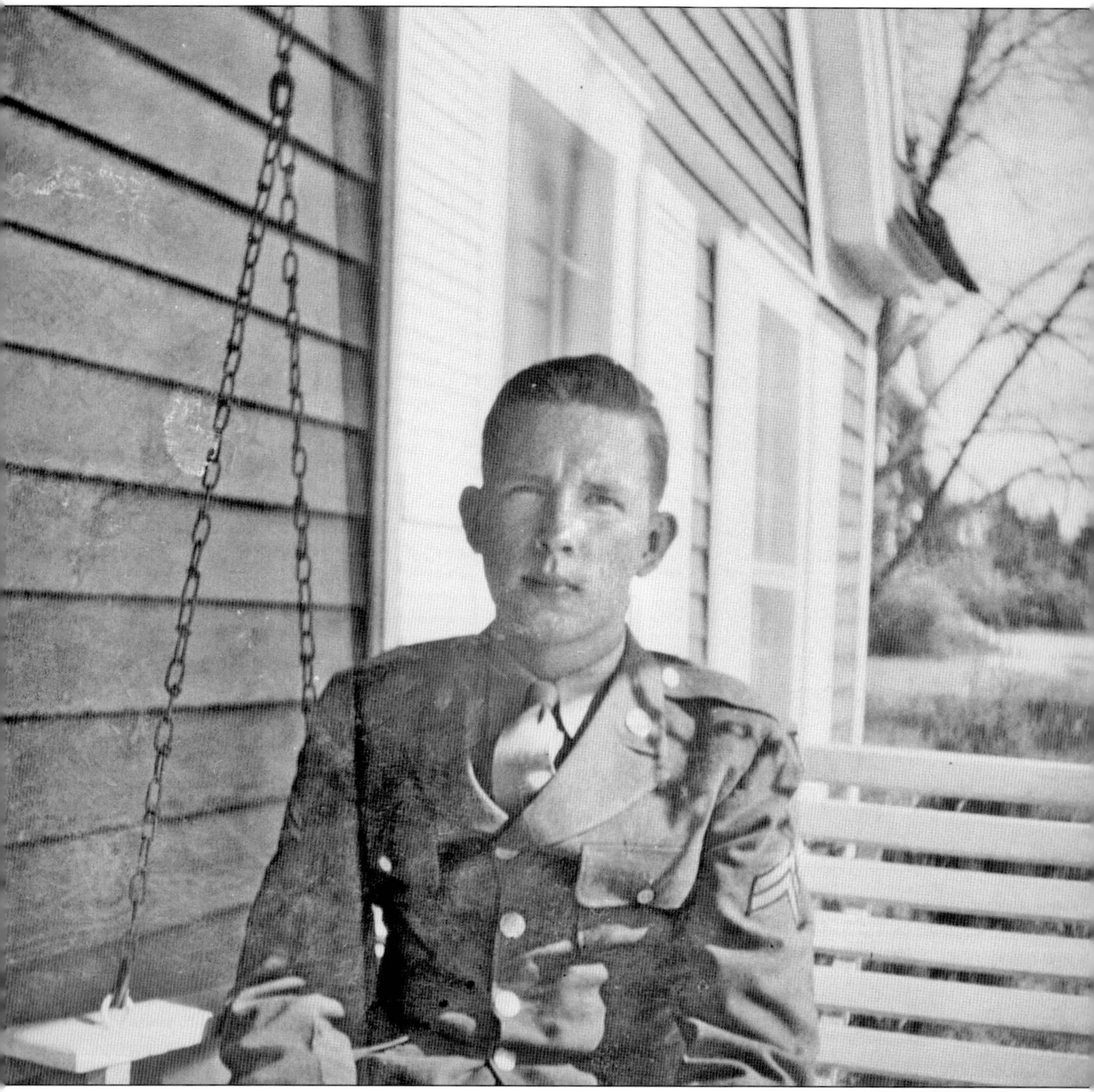

Bobby Gordon was photographed in his uniform on a porch swing. After he graduated from college in 1943, he served with the 106th Cavalry in Europe.

Five

Friends in the Neighborhood

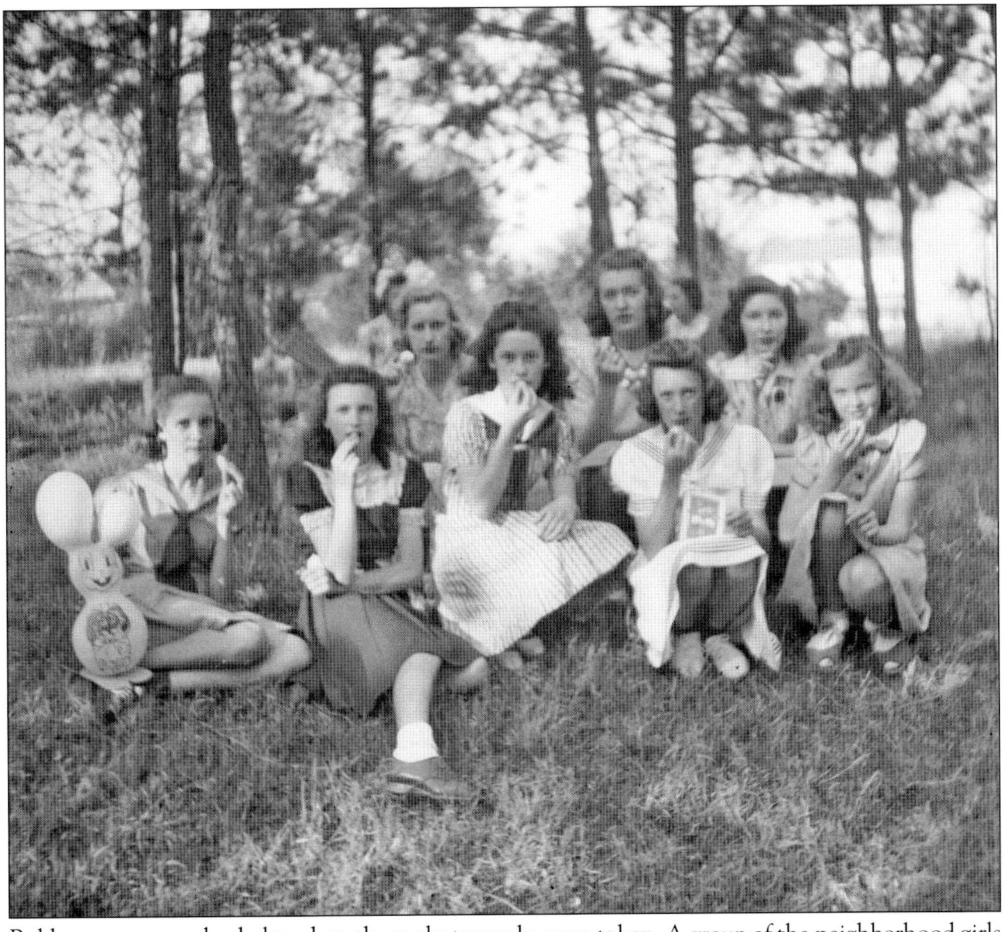

Bobby was a young bachelor when these photographs were taken. A group of the neighborhood girls enjoyed posing for him, sometimes with interesting results, such as this photograph that probably has an Easter theme. The girls are, from left to right, Mary Ann Gordon, unidentified, Anita Chandler, Joy Ann Downs, Charlotte Jackson, unidentified, Mary Ashford, and ? Nicholson.

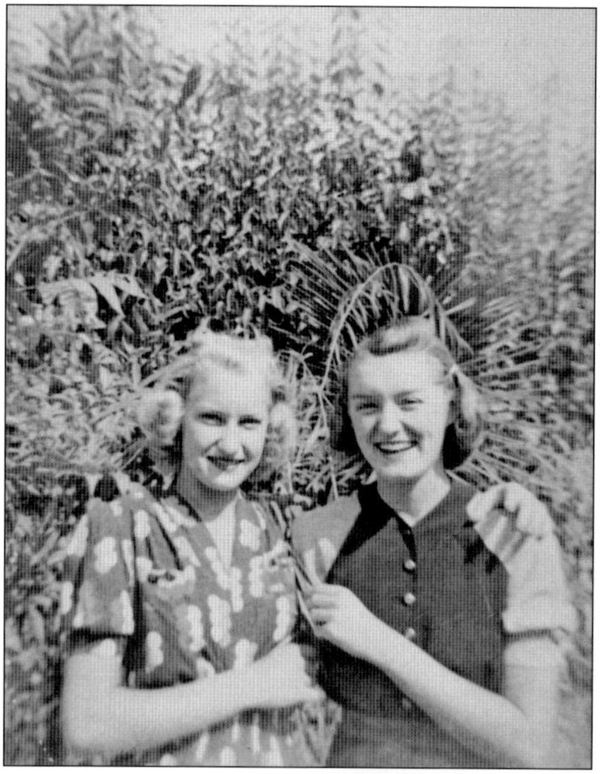

Pictured at left, Anita Chandler (left) and Charlotte Jackson were both related to Bobby Gordon; their mothers were sisters to Bobby's mother. Charlotte's family owned the Fain house before R.E. Fain. She eventually moved to Arizona. Below, Charlotte (left) and Anita relax in the shade in front of the Gordon duplex. They show a slice of life from 1930s–1940s Watkinsville.

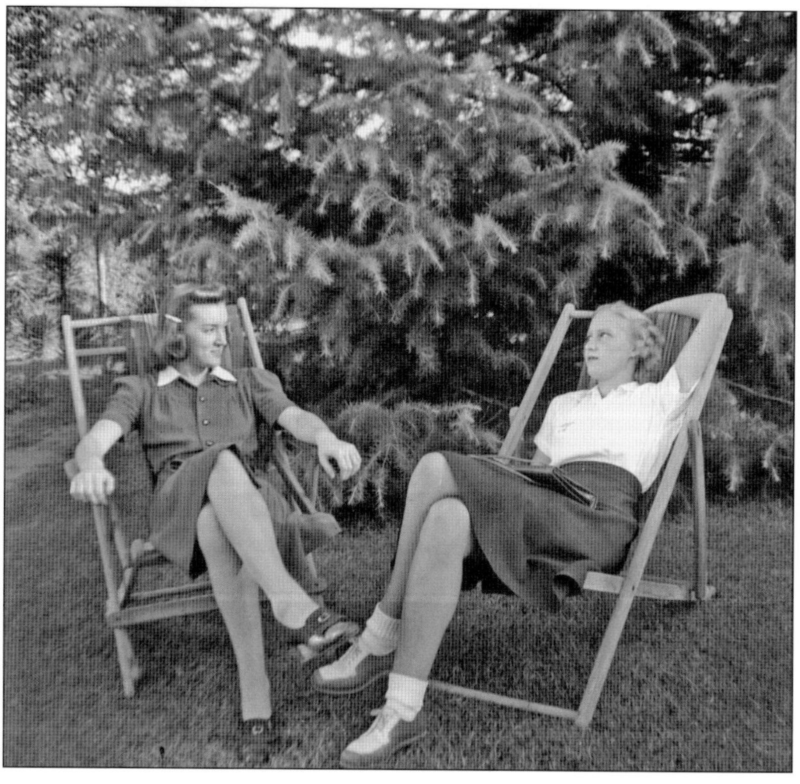

From left to right, Mary Ashford, Anita Chandler, and Joan Camp dress for a chilly day. Bobby Gordon, Joan Camp, Anita Chandler, and Mary Ashford all lived within a block of each other. These photographs show that they spent a lot of time together.

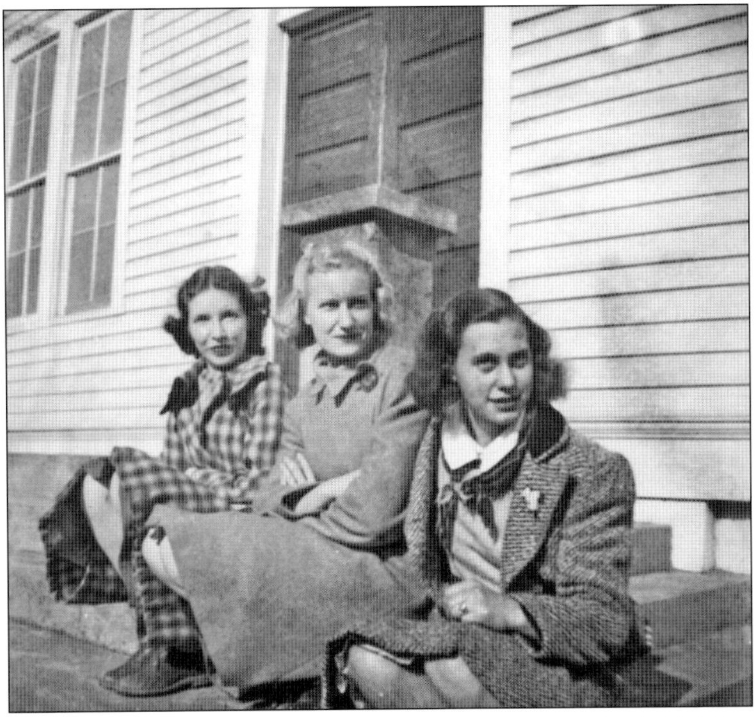

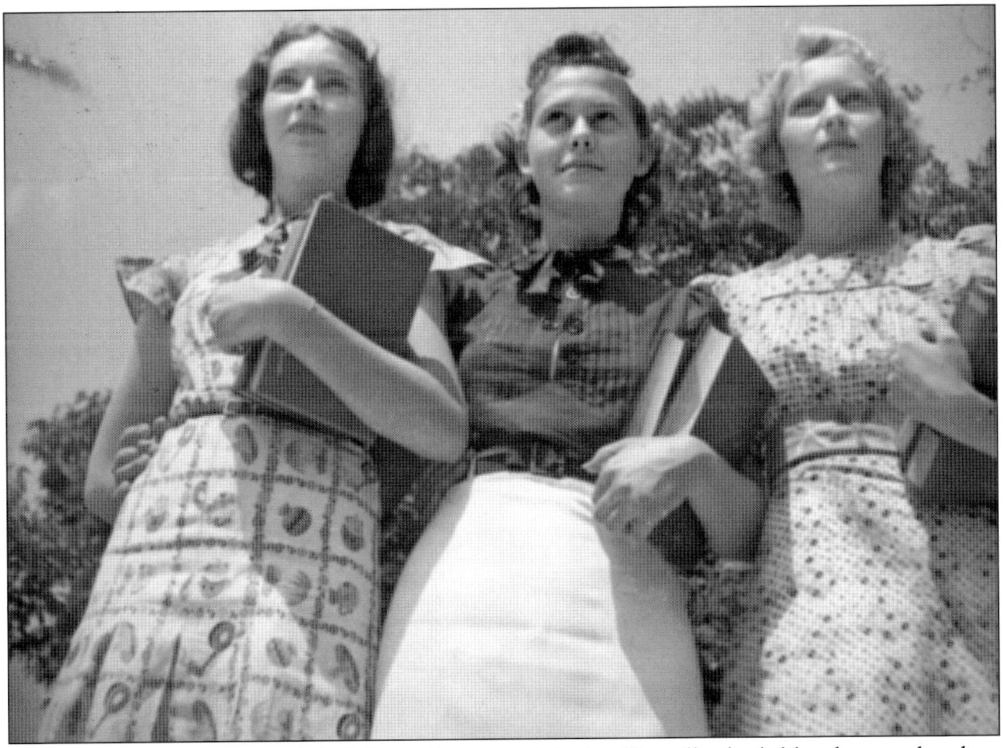

From left to right, Mary Ashford, Joan Camp, and Anita Chandler look like they are heading off to school. They were all members of the Oconee High School class of 1940 who had been together since kindergarten.

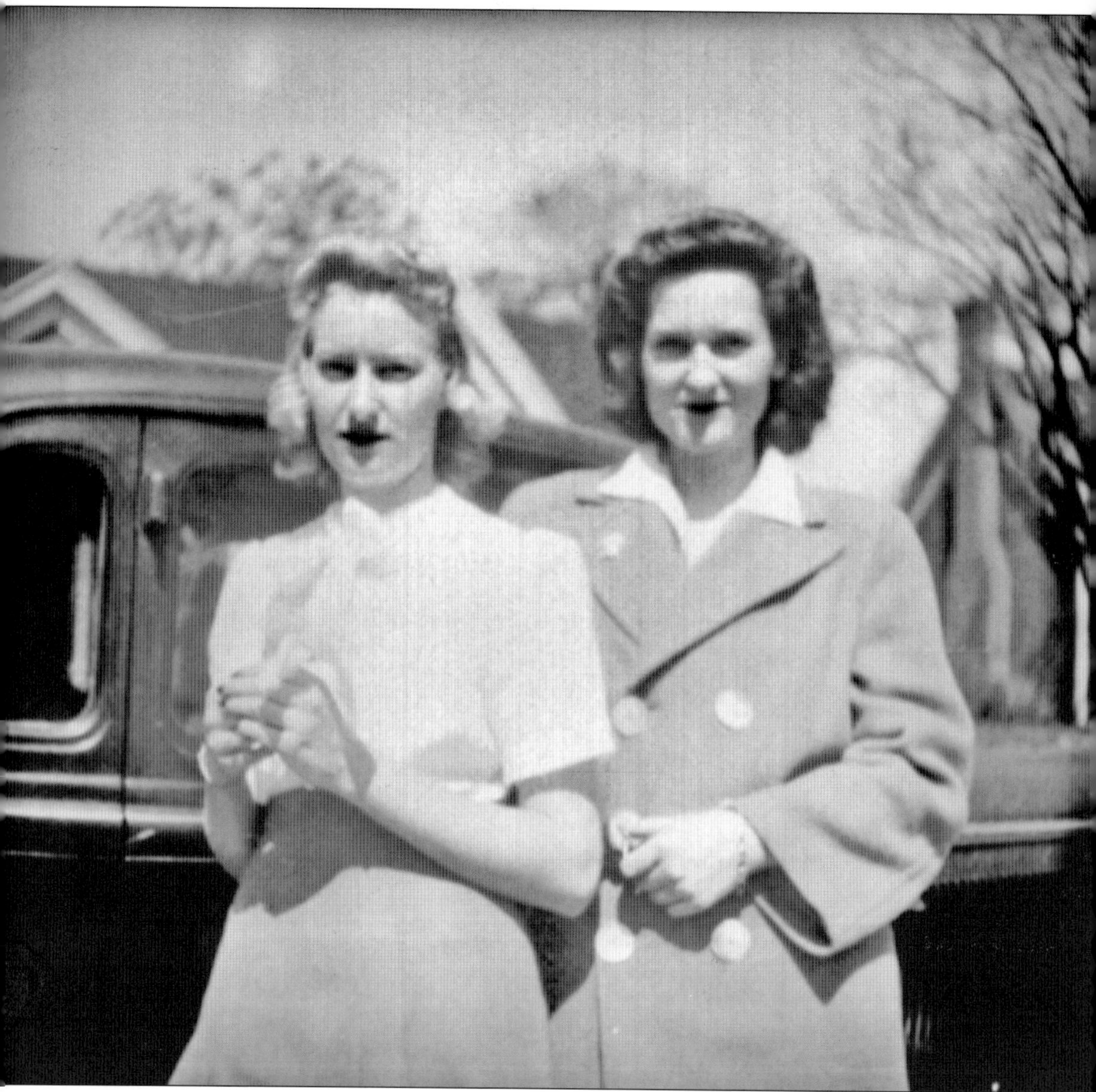

Anita Chandler (left) and Elma Anthony pose in front of the old Gordon home on Main Street for Bobby's camera.

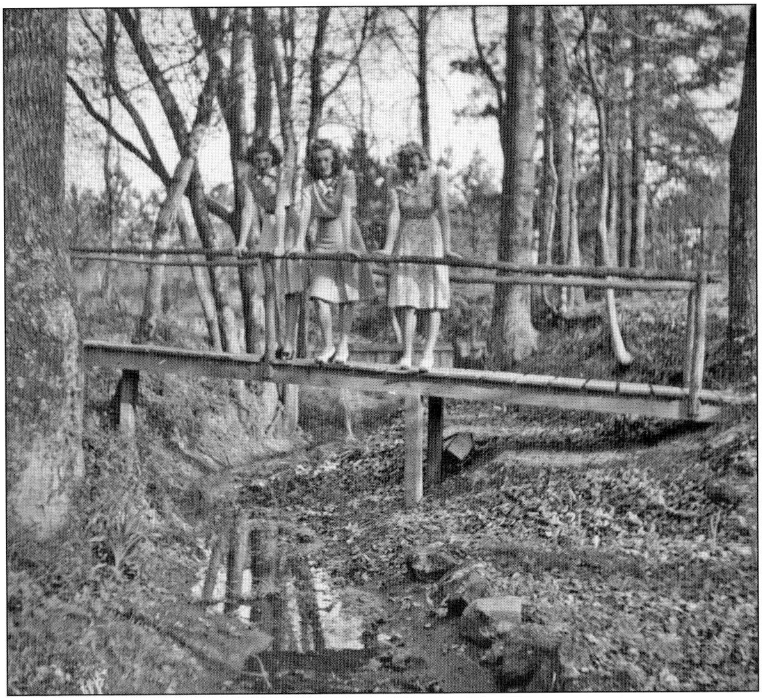

The three girls on this bridge are, from left to right, unidentified, Charlotte Jackson, and Anita Chandler. These photographs were taken along the creek behind the Fain and Ashford homes. Below, Anita Chandler is swinging near the creek in the same area.

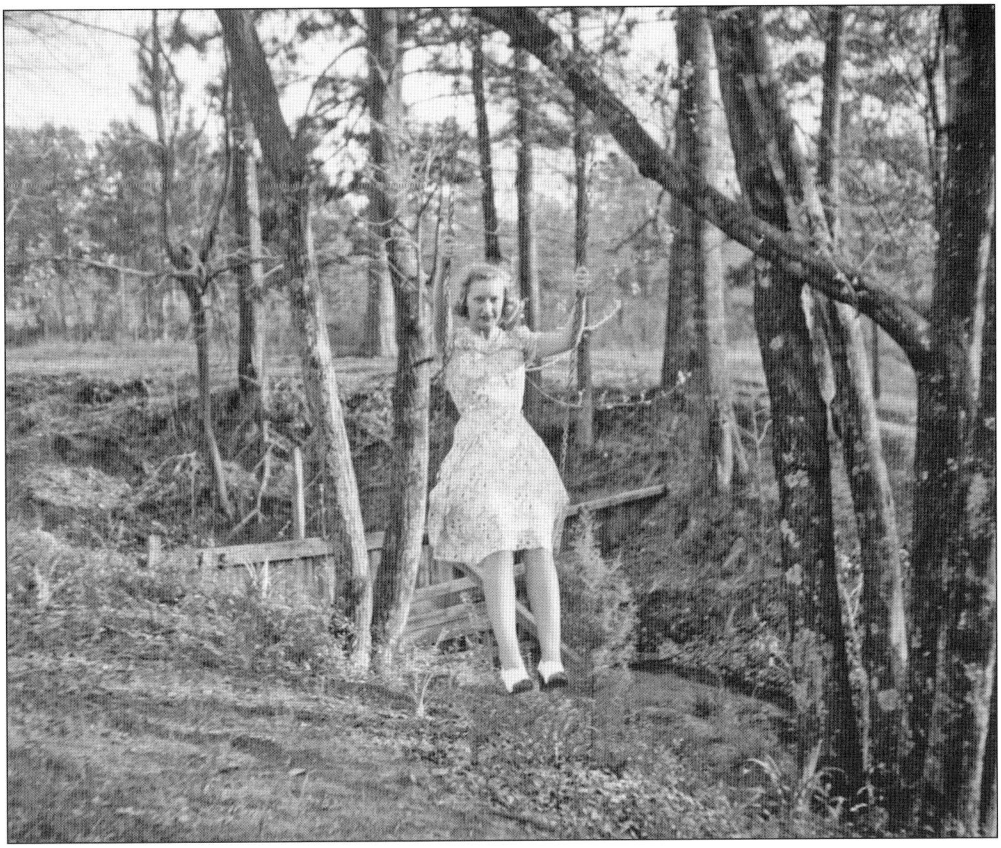

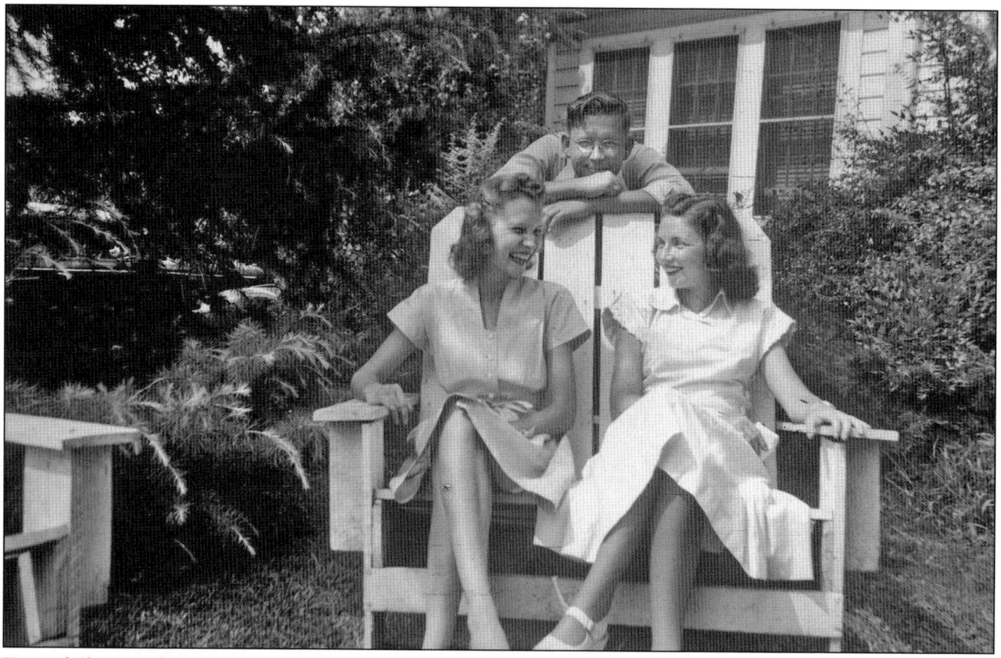

From left to right, Mary Ann Gordon, Bobby Gordon, and Mary Ashford have gathered on the large chair outside the duplex where the Gordon family lived. This is an example of a photograph in which Bobby used a timer so he could be in the picture.

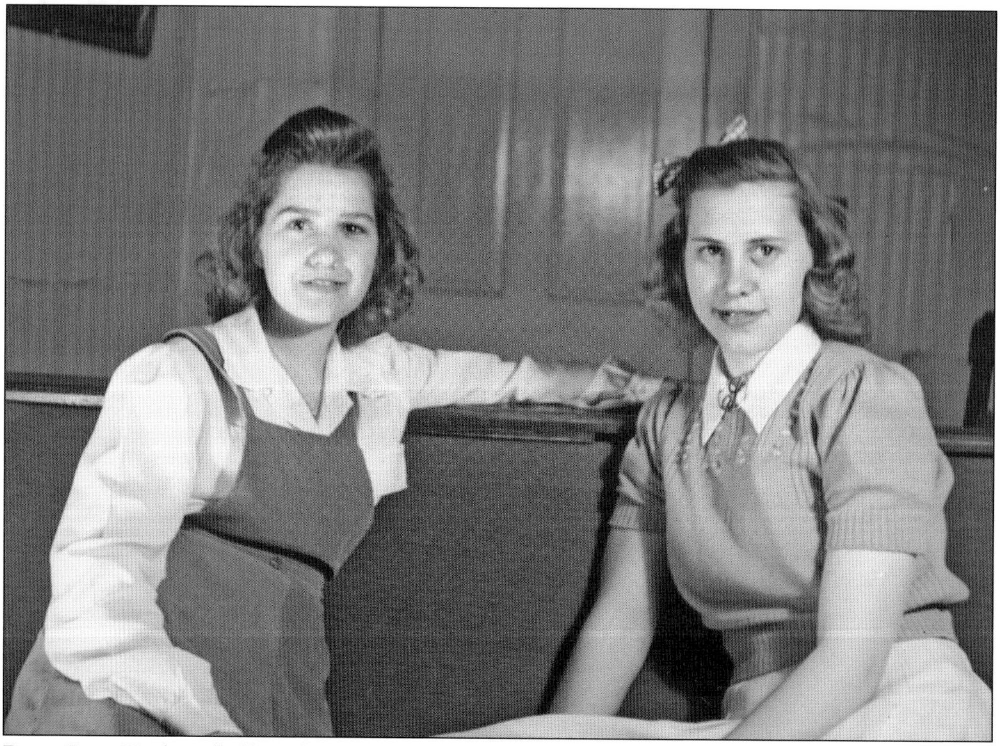

Betty Jean Hodges (left) and Joan Camp pose for Bobby. They both graduated from Oconee County High School in 1940.

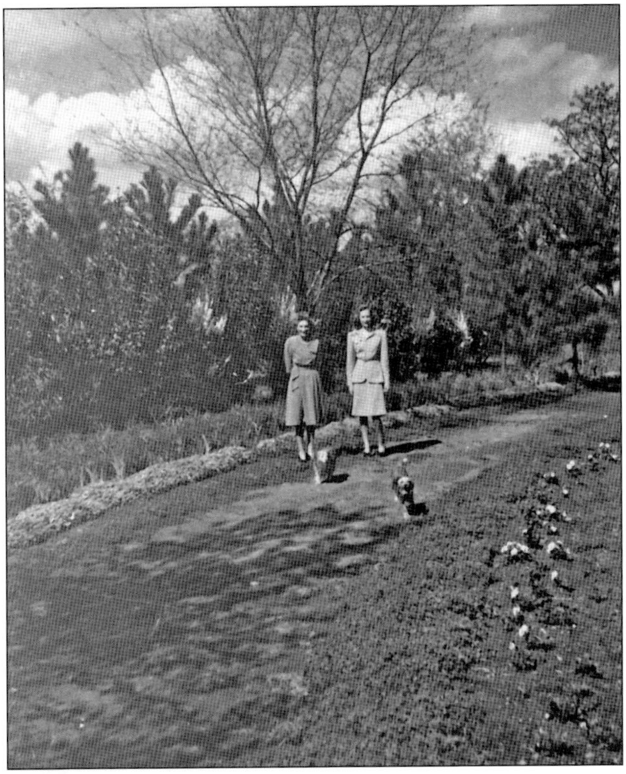

At right, Martha Fain and her niece Mary Ann Gordon walk the dogs in the Fains' front yard. Martha was well known for her gardens. Below, Mary Ann is standing among Martha's tulips.

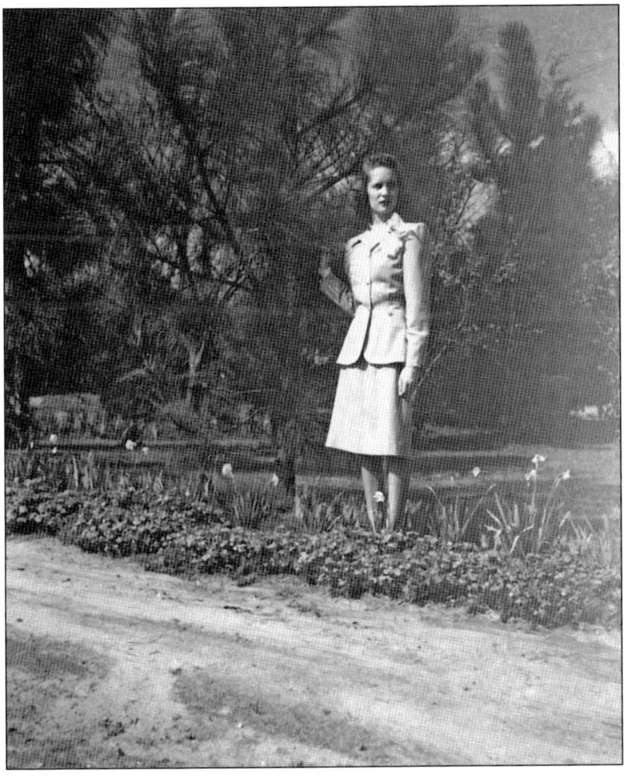

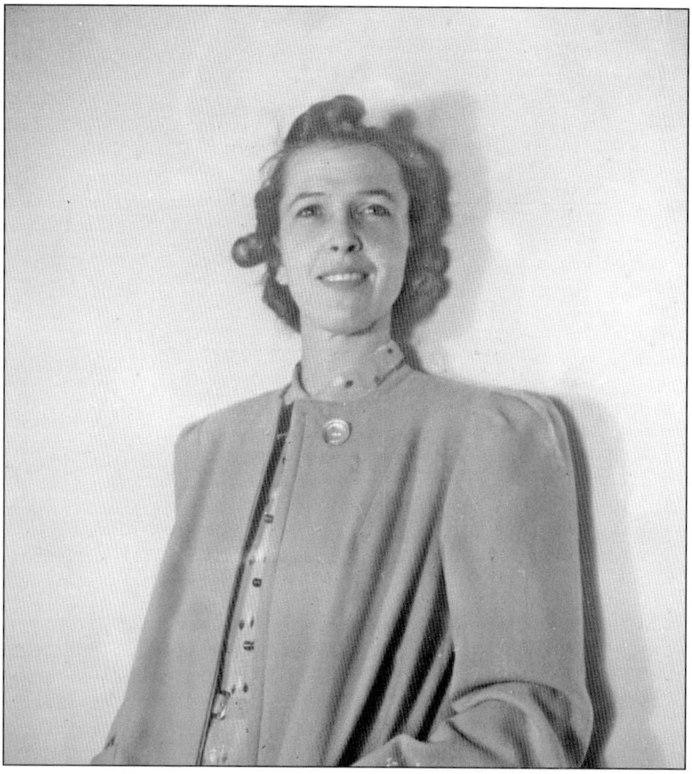

At left is Sara Bell, who married Julian Aiken. Below is Mary Ruth Camp, the sister of Joan Camp. She was a member of the Oconee High School class of 1941.

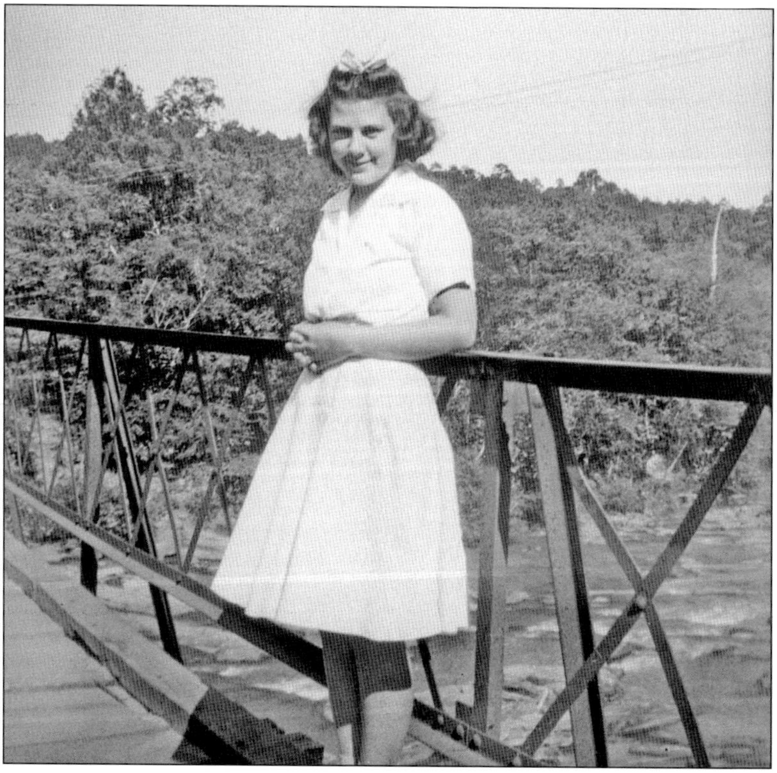

The college banner reads "GSGW" for Georgia State College for Women. The college began in Milledgeville in 1889 as the two-year Georgia Normal and Industrial College. It became a four-year college in 1917, and its name was changed to the Georgia State College for Women in 1922. Today, it is known as Georgia College. The girl in the photograph is unidentified.

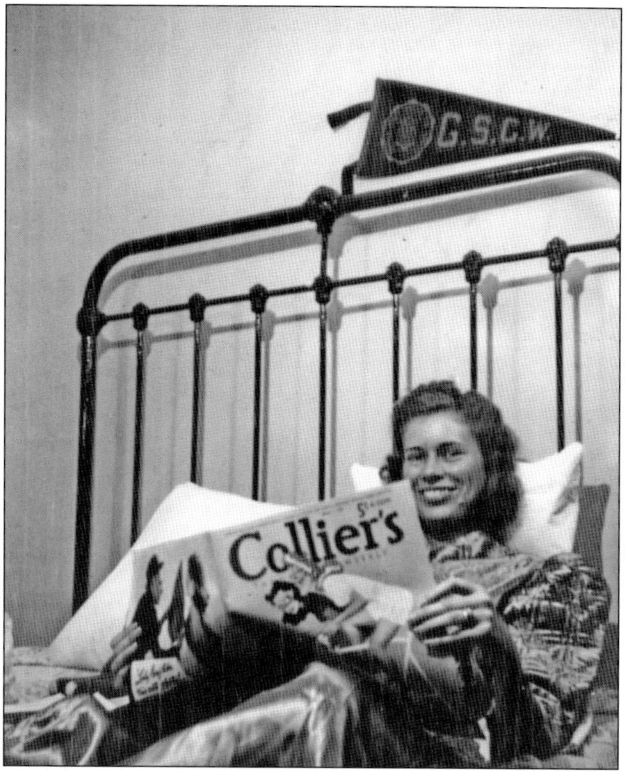

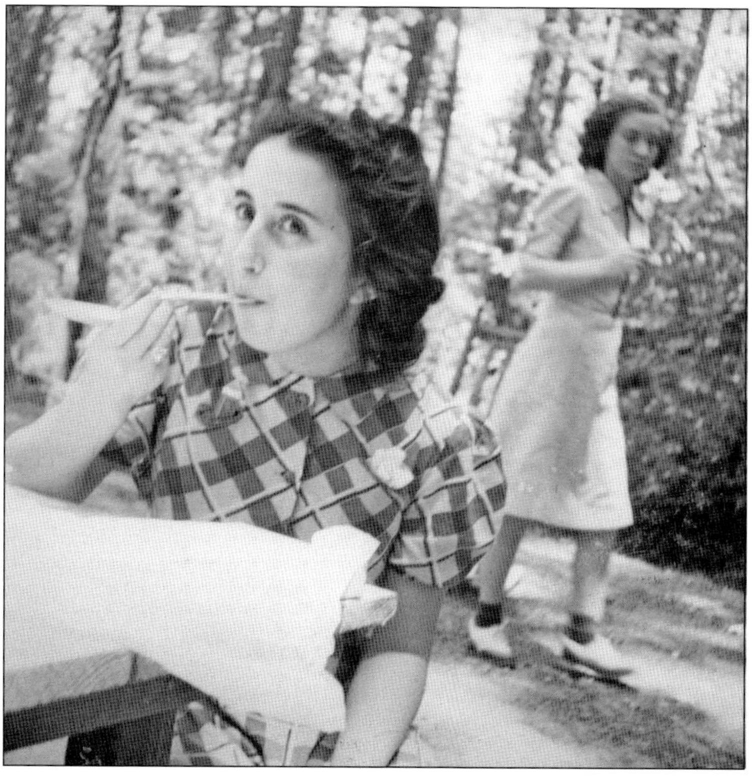

Bobby caught Frances Saxon (left) and an unidentified friend at a picnic. The Saxon home, which was on the south side of today's Jackson and Main Streets, is one of the town's lovingly restored homes. Frances graduated from Oconee High School in 1940.

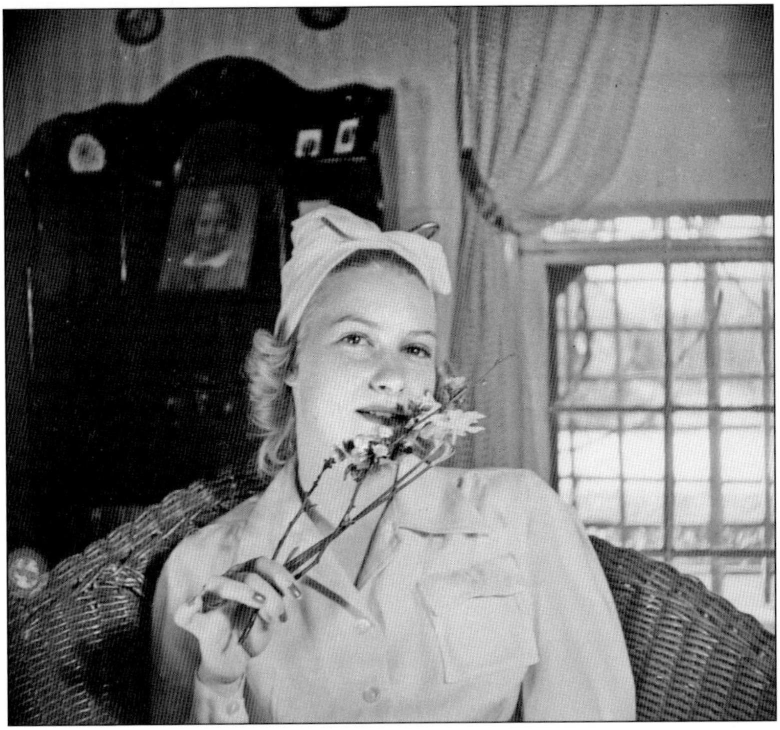

Anita Osborne Chandler played basketball while in high school and went to college out of state. Martha Fain was her aunt. Her mother, Anne Osborne Chandler, was a twin sister to Mary Osborne Gordon, Bobby's mother. Although Anita married and lived out of state, she used to return for high school reunions.

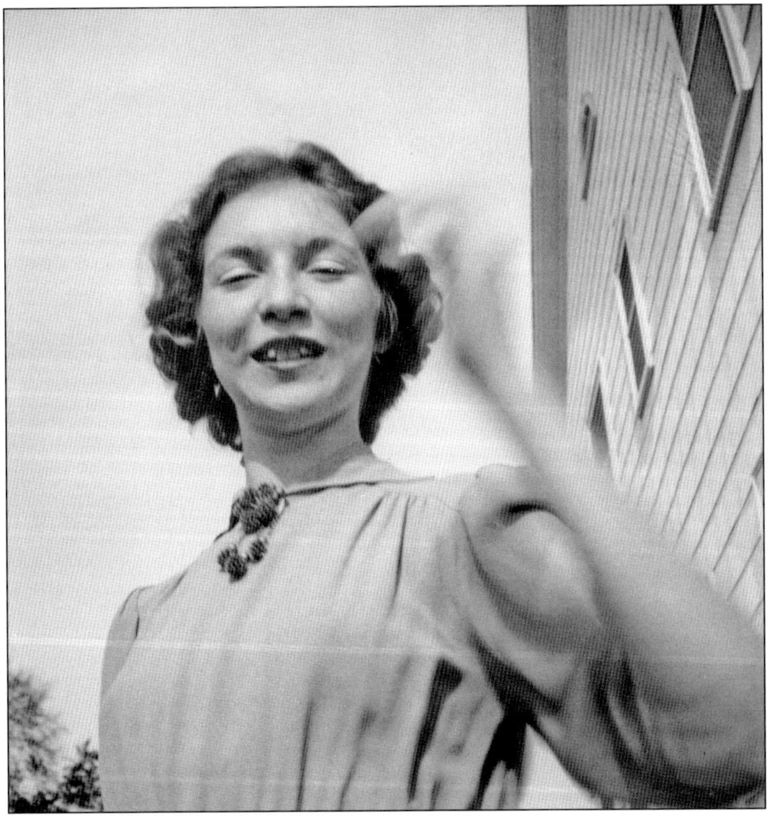

Mary Ashford went to the University of North Carolina and became an administrator in a doctor's office.

Joan Camp was a member of the Oconee High School class of 1940. After she graduated from high school, she got a government job in Washington, DC.

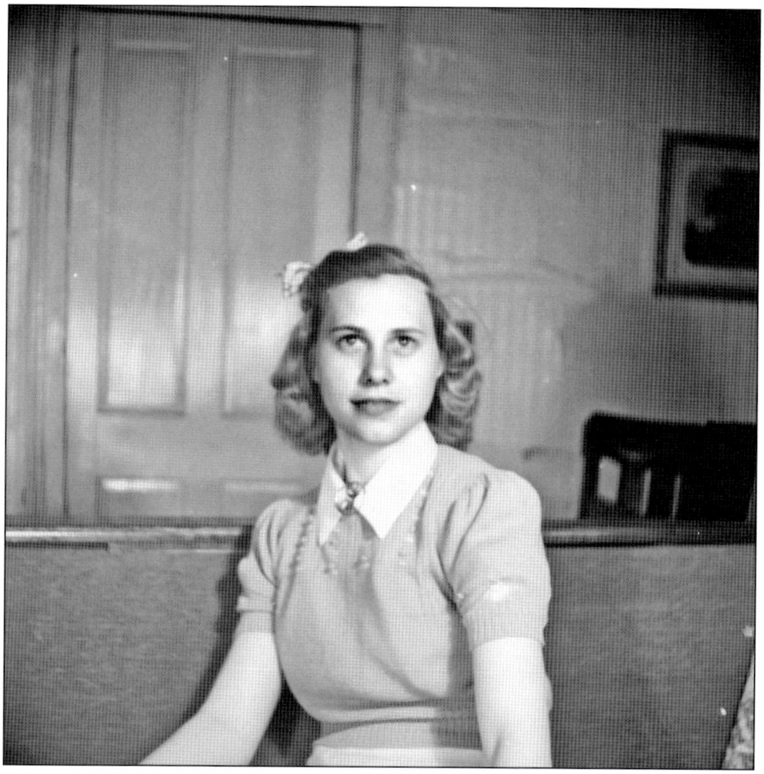

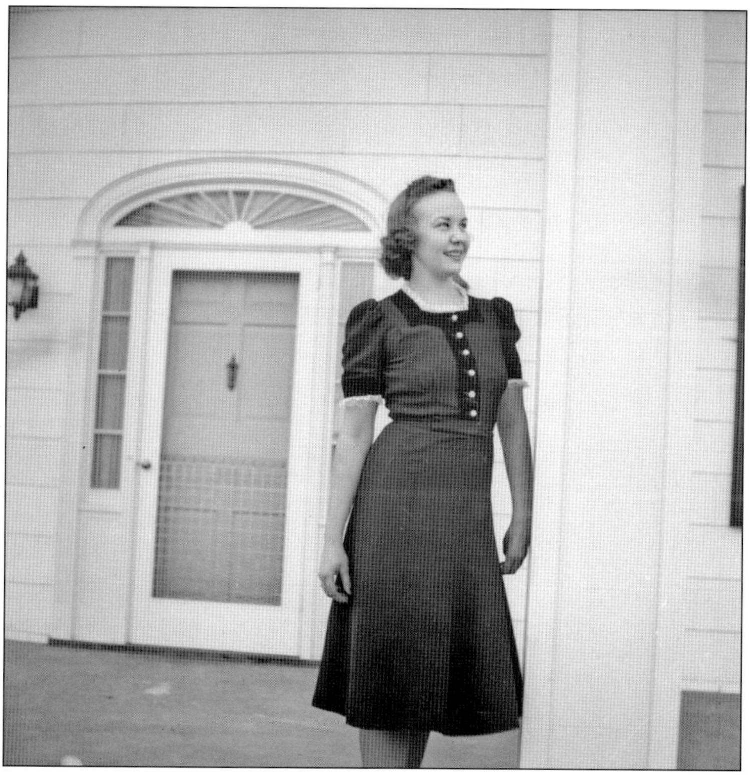

Bobby photographed Catherine Chandler on her aunt's front porch several times. Catherine played basketball in high school and graduated in 1936.

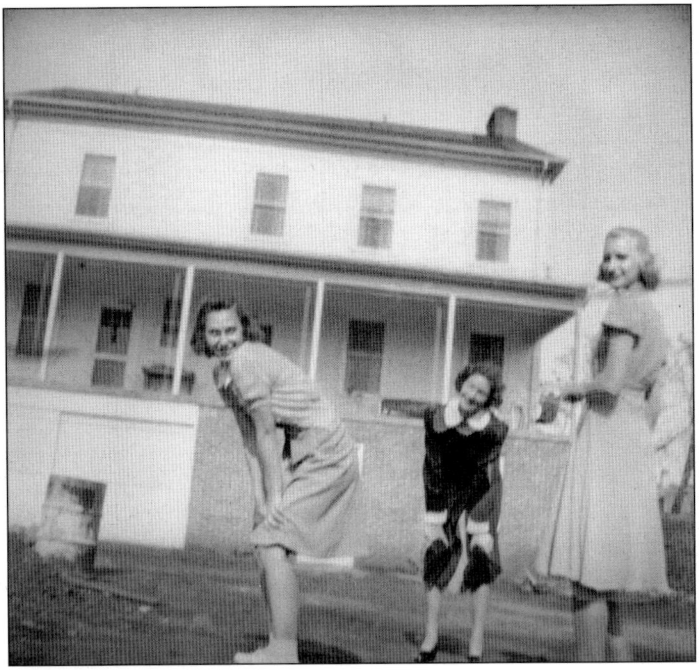

One beautiful day, Bobby and his friends decided to use his camera to illustrate current hit songs. These photographs are the result. From left to right, Joan Camp, Mary Ashford, and Anita Chandler discuss how to illustrate "I Get a Kick out of You."

Anita (left) and Joan switched places for this photograph. "I Get a Kick out of You" was a Cole Porter song from the 1934 Broadway musical *Anything Goes*.

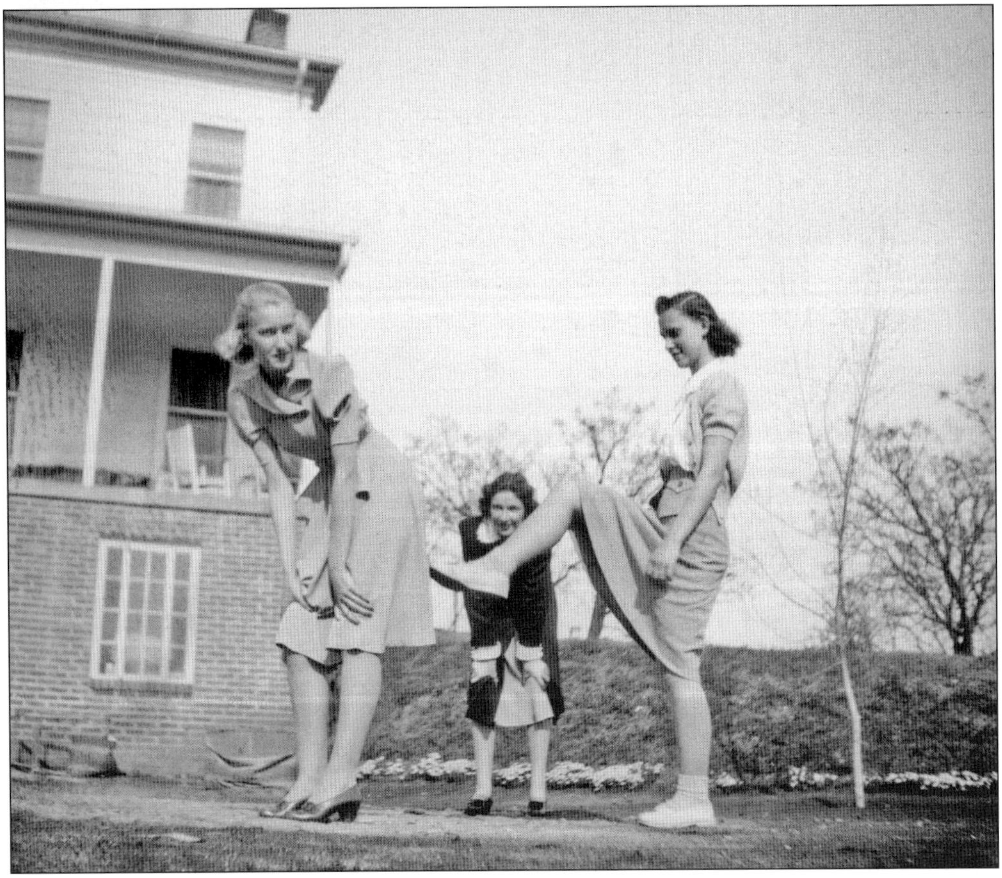

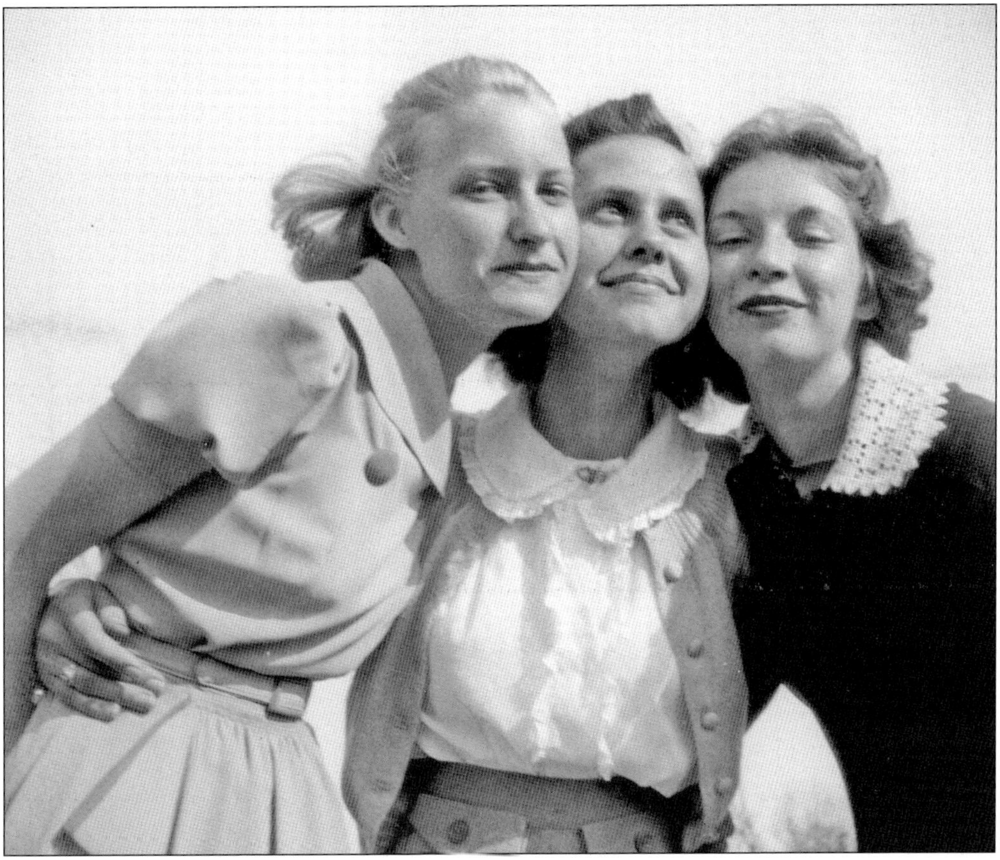

From left to right, Anita Chandler, Joan Camp, and Mary Ashford illustrate Irving Berlin's "Dancing Cheek to Cheek," which was the number-one song in 1935. It was from the movie *Top Hat*.

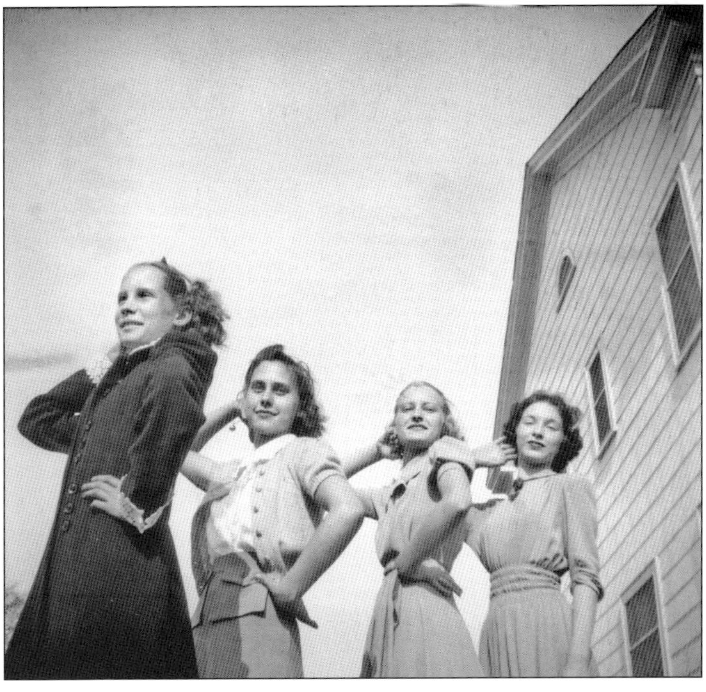

From left to right, Mary Ann Gordon joins Joan Camp, Anita Chandler, and Mary Ashford to illustrate "Chattanooga Choo Choo," the number-one song in 1941. It was written by Mack Gordon and Harry Warren and recorded by Glenn Miller and his orchestra. It was in the movie *Sun Valley Serenade*.

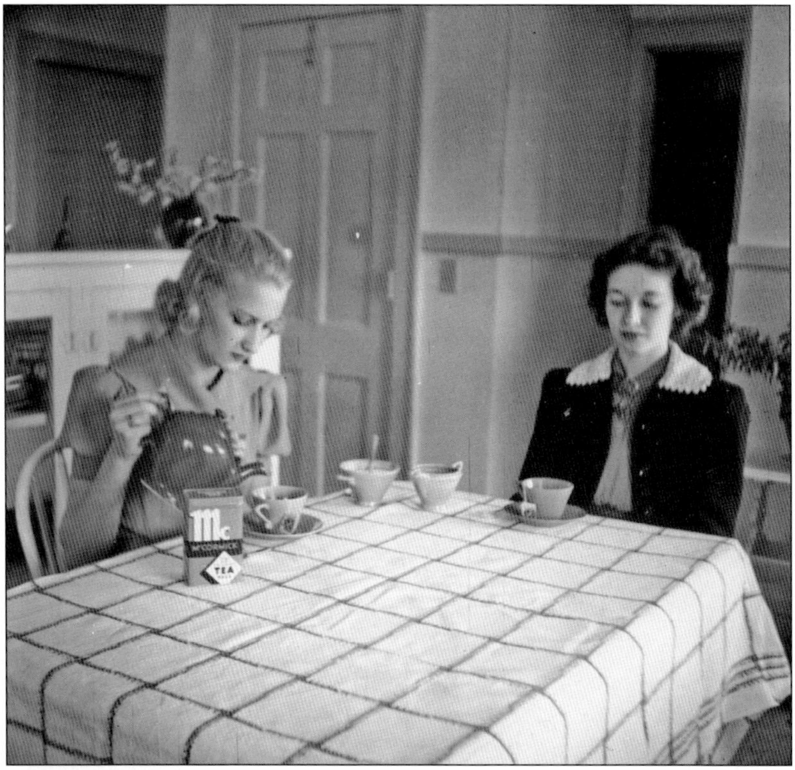

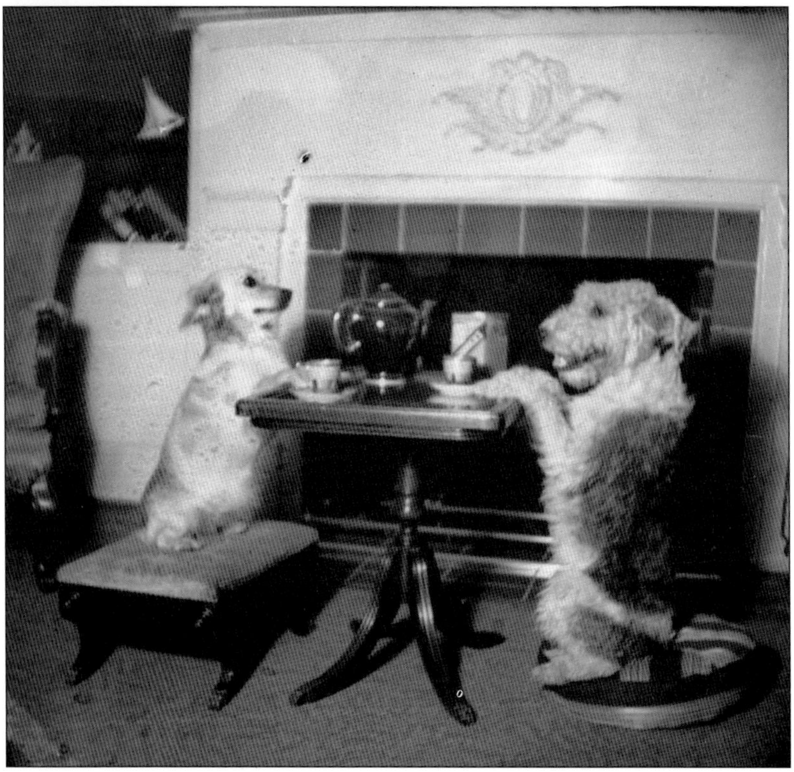

Bobby and his friends created two photographs portraying the 1925 hit "Tea for Two" from the musical *No No Nanette*. The lyrics were by Irving Berlin, and the music by Vincent Youmans. At top, Anita Chandler is pouring tea for Mary Ashford. A version of "Tea for Two" was recorded in 1939 by Fats Waller, and another was recorded by Bing Crosby and Connie Boswell in 1940. At bottom, the dogs joining in on the fun belonged to R.E. Fain.

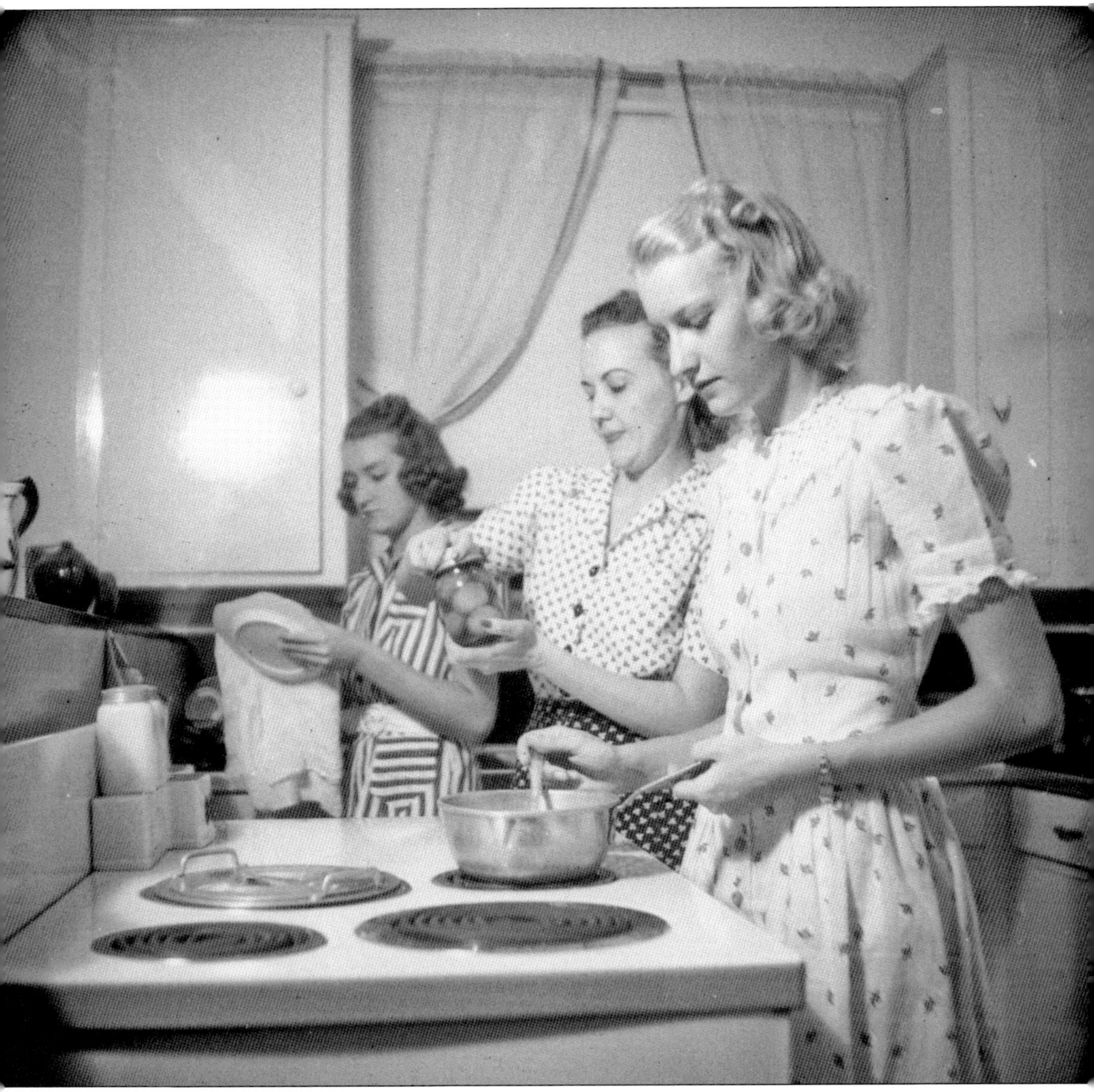

Pictured are three girls in the kitchen of the Fain home, (from left to right) Charlotte Jackson, Catherine "Cat" Chandler, and Anita Chandler. The jar Cat is opening probably contained fruit canned at the community canning plant. The plant, in an old dilapidated house near the county jail, was moved to the new Agriculture and Home Economics Building on the Oconee High School campus in 1939. Ellis Garrett, the newly hired agriculture teacher, remembers acquiring a large used wood-fired boiler and some stored canning equipment that the University of Georgia was not using to get the new plant started. He thought it was the "largest and best equipped canning plant in the country." This was important, because most people raised their own fruits, meats, and vegetables. No one had home freezers, and electricity was just making it out into the rural areas of the county.

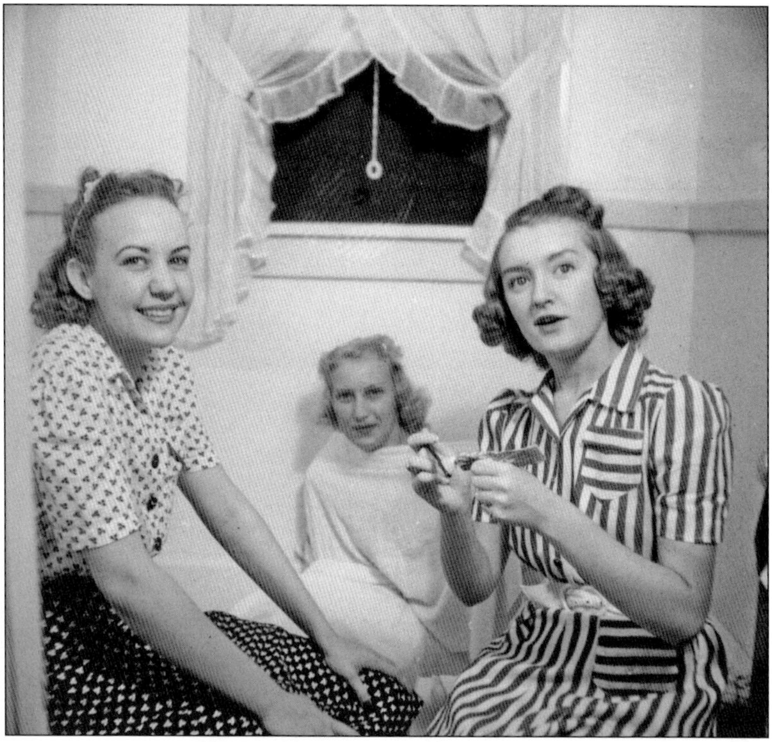

At left, from left to right, Cat Chandler, Anita Chandler, and Charlotte Jackson apply makeup, possibly to get ready for a social gathering. Below, from left to right, Anita Chandler, an unidentified man, and Charlotte Jackson share a drink.

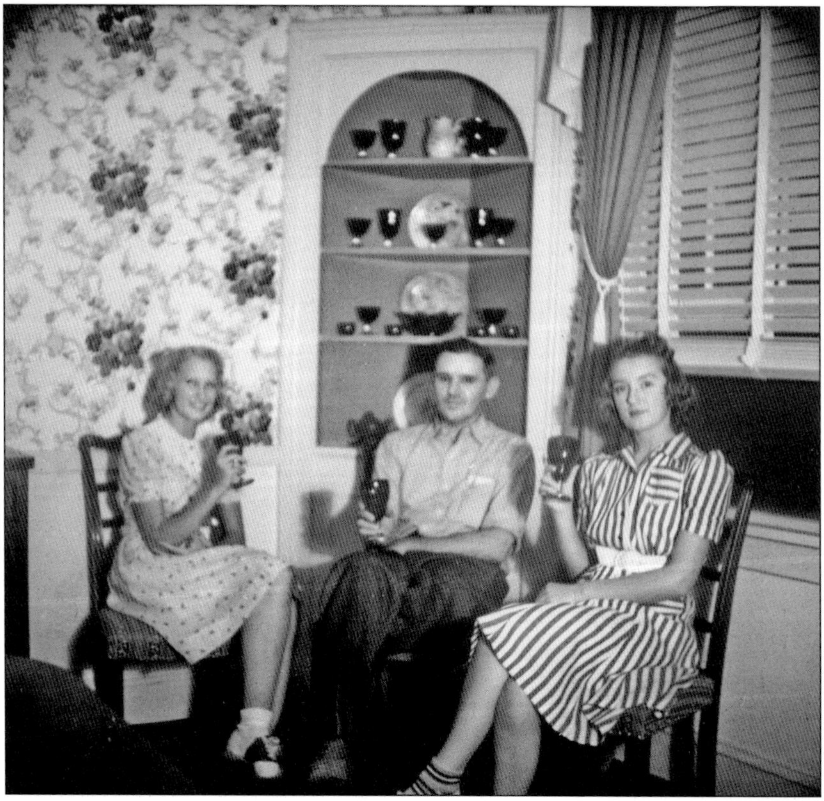

Six

Children and Animals

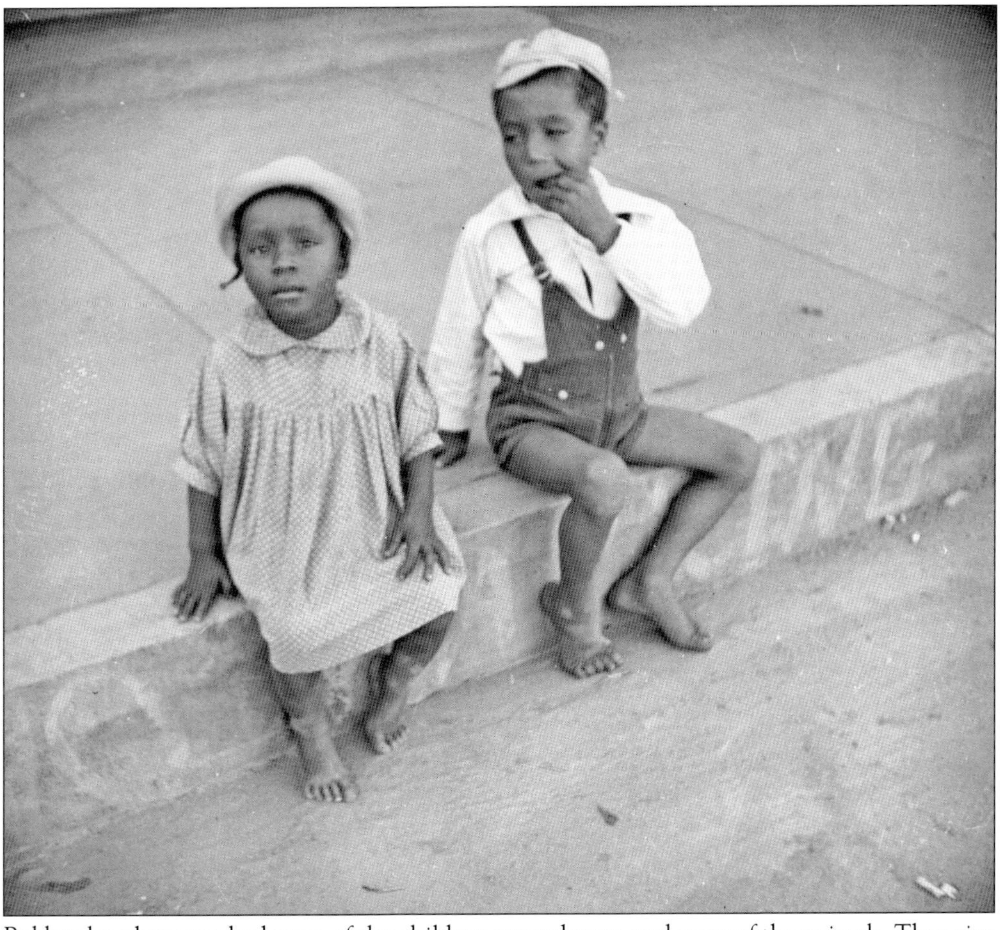

Bobby also photographed some of the children around town and some of the animals. They give a picture of Watkinsville life even when no one knows who many of the children are. These two barefoot youngsters are sitting on the Main Street sidewalk.

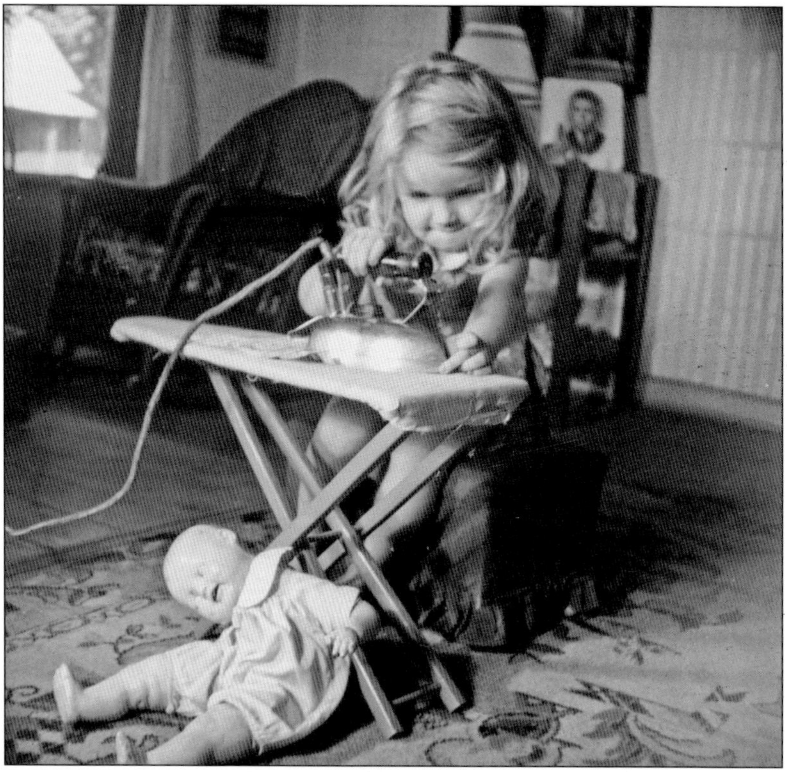

Bobby's people skills brought out the best in his subjects. Both of these images are of Sarah Harriet Shankle. At left, she is hard at work playing with her toys, and below, she is showing off her lovely dress.

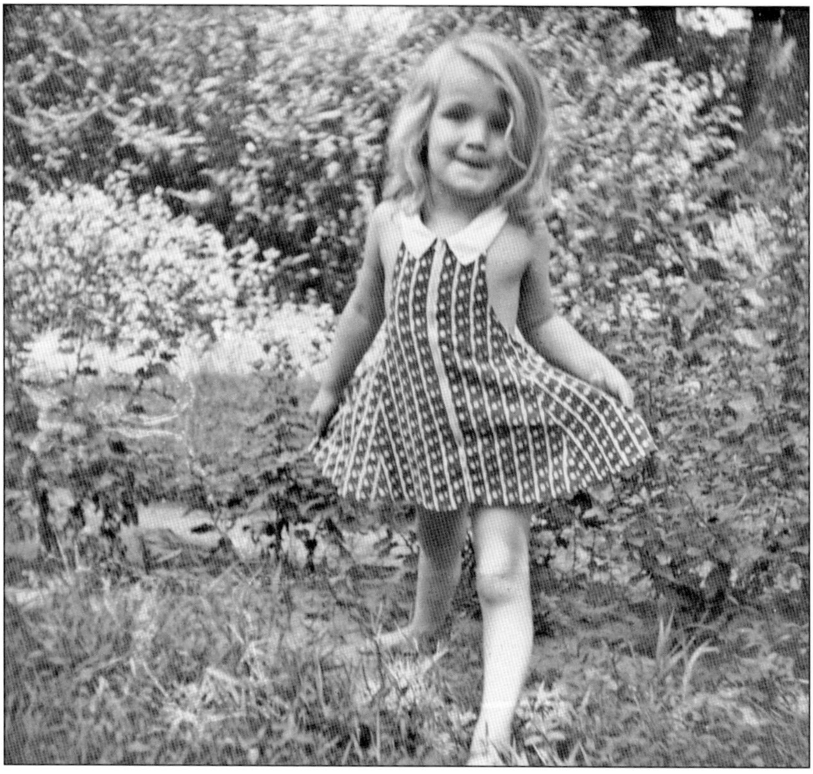

Although R.E. Fain and his wife, Martha, did not have any children, this youngster appears to be on friendly terms with R.E. The photograph was taken on the front stairs of the Fain home.

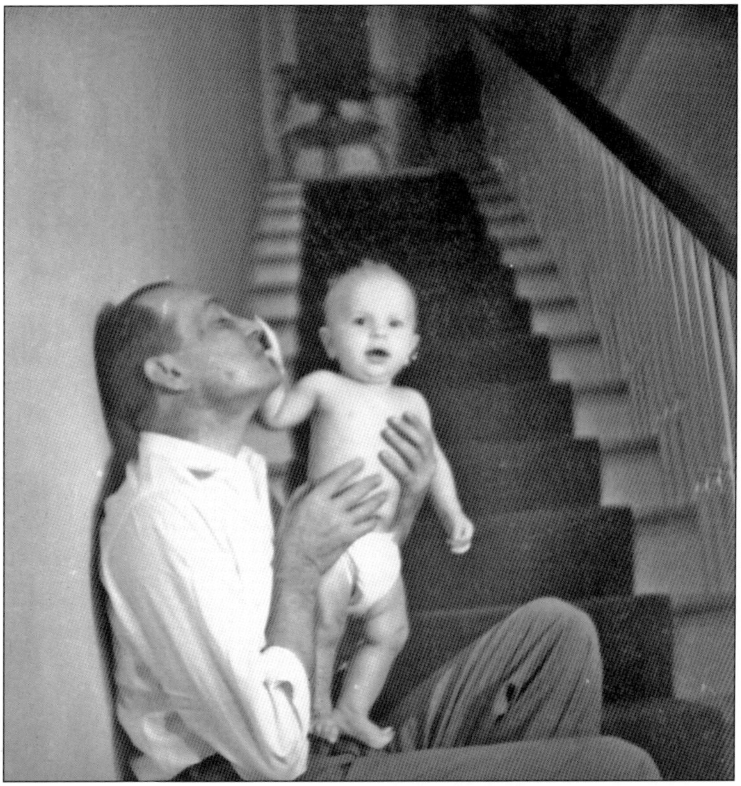

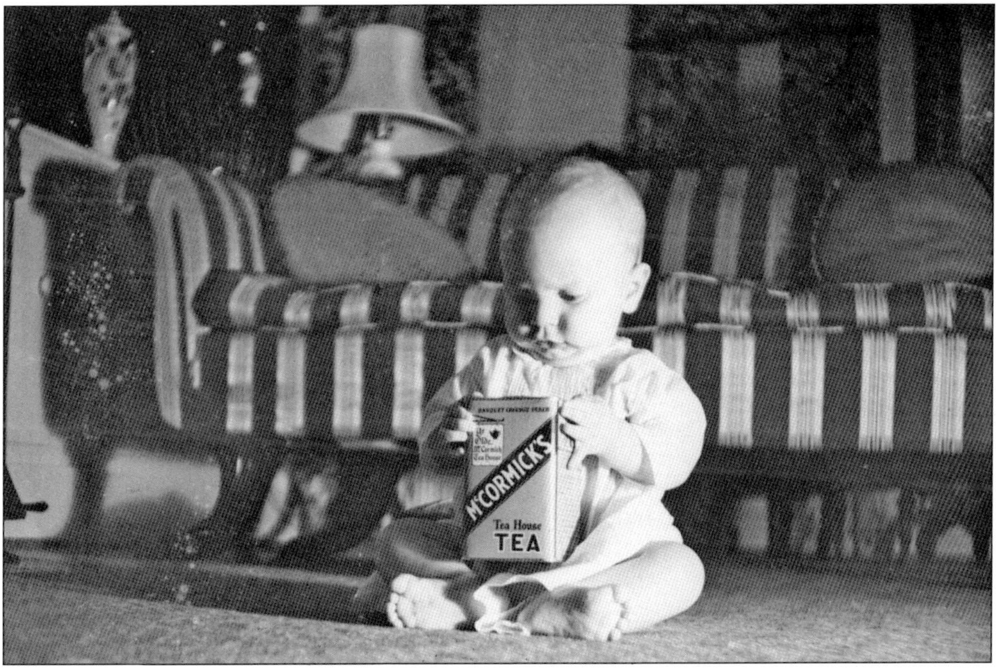

R.E. Fain was a salesman for McCormick's Tea company. The company was founded by Willoughby M. McCormick in 1881. It began selling tea in 1905 and was one of the earliest companies to sell tea in small gauze bags.

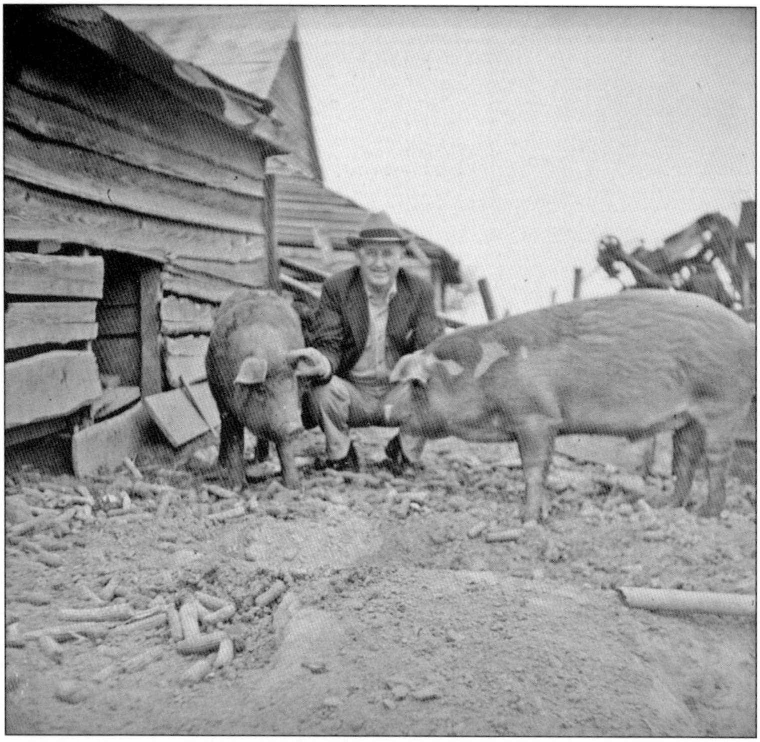

Nathan Warren Aiken was a farmer and a blacksmith. He also drove a school bus. His route covered the Flat Rock area where he lived. The unpaved dirt roads made this a challenging job when it rained.

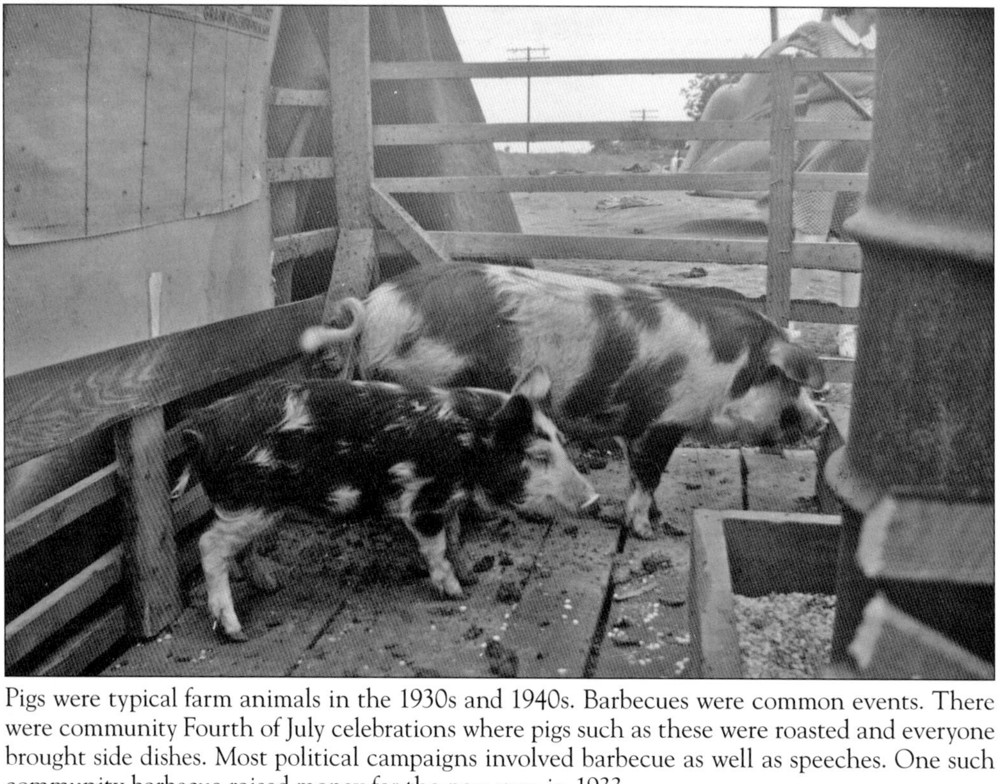

Pigs were typical farm animals in the 1930s and 1940s. Barbecues were common events. There were community Fourth of July celebrations where pigs such as these were roasted and everyone brought side dishes. Most political campaigns involved barbecue as well as speeches. One such community barbecue raised money for the new gym in 1933.

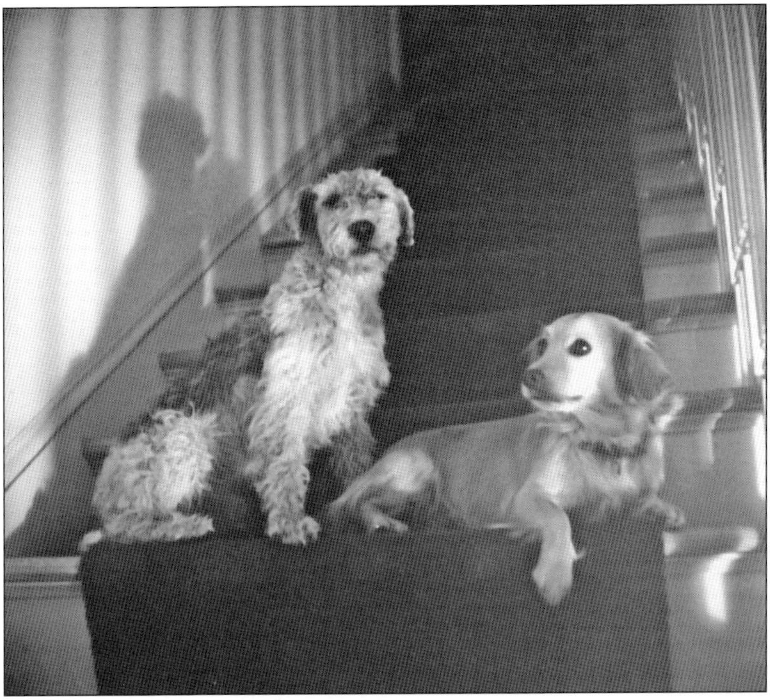

The Fains' dogs pose for Bobby at home. The photograph below gives an excellent view of the lovely staircase just inside the front door of the Fain home as well as a 1930s fan.

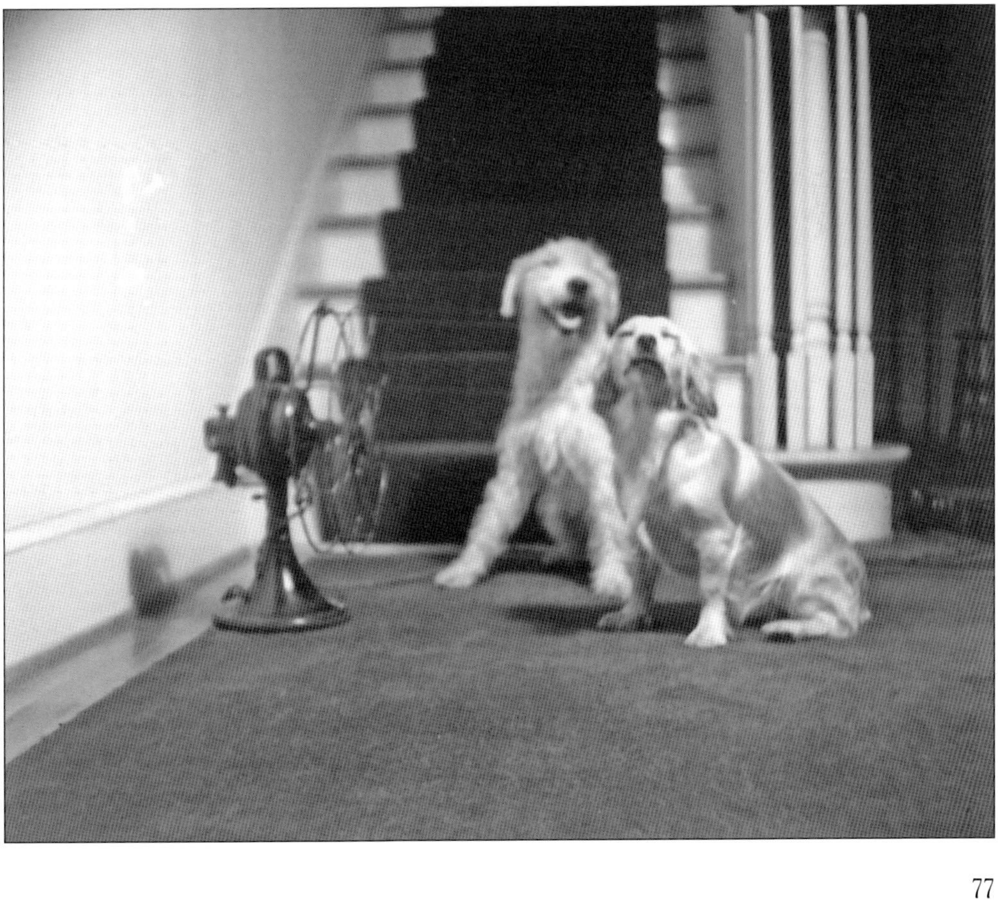

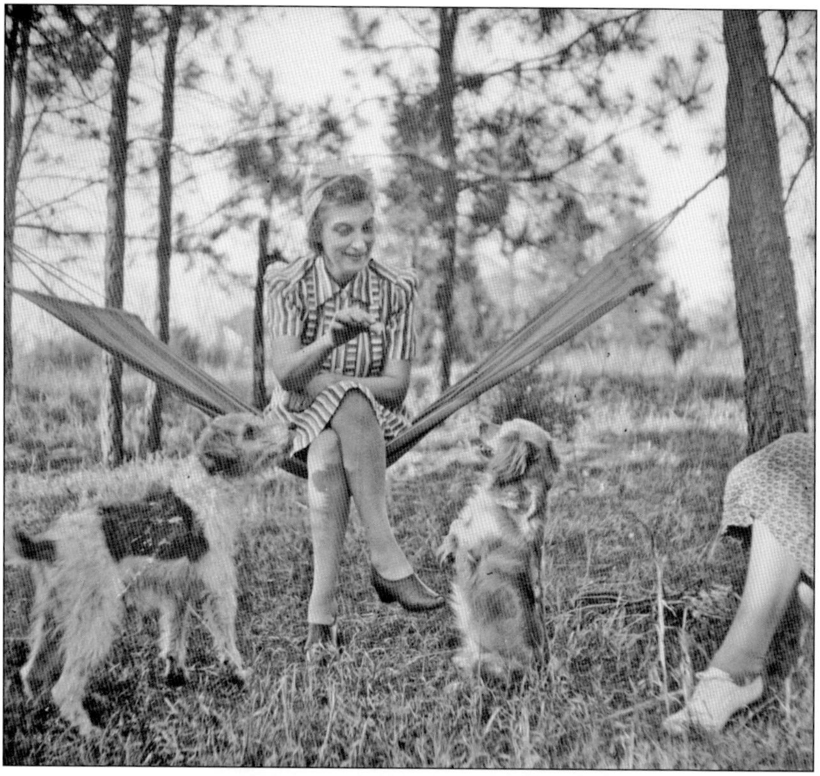

Martha Fain is pictured with her dogs.

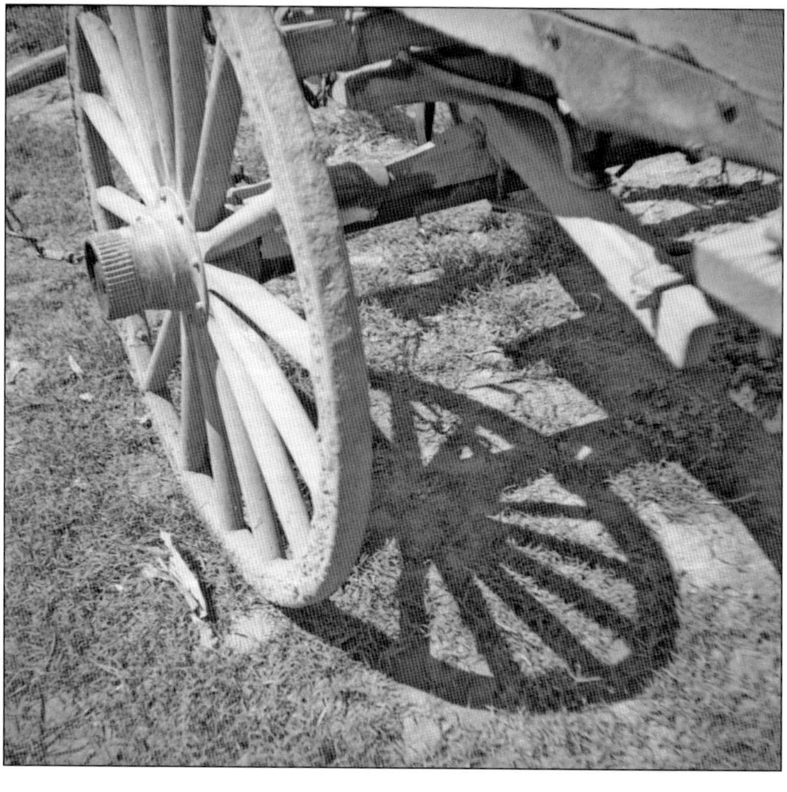

Bobby liked to experiment with shadows. Several photographs in the collection show the results, like this excellent example of Bobby's artistic skills and his willingness to experiment with his camera.

Seven

FAMILY

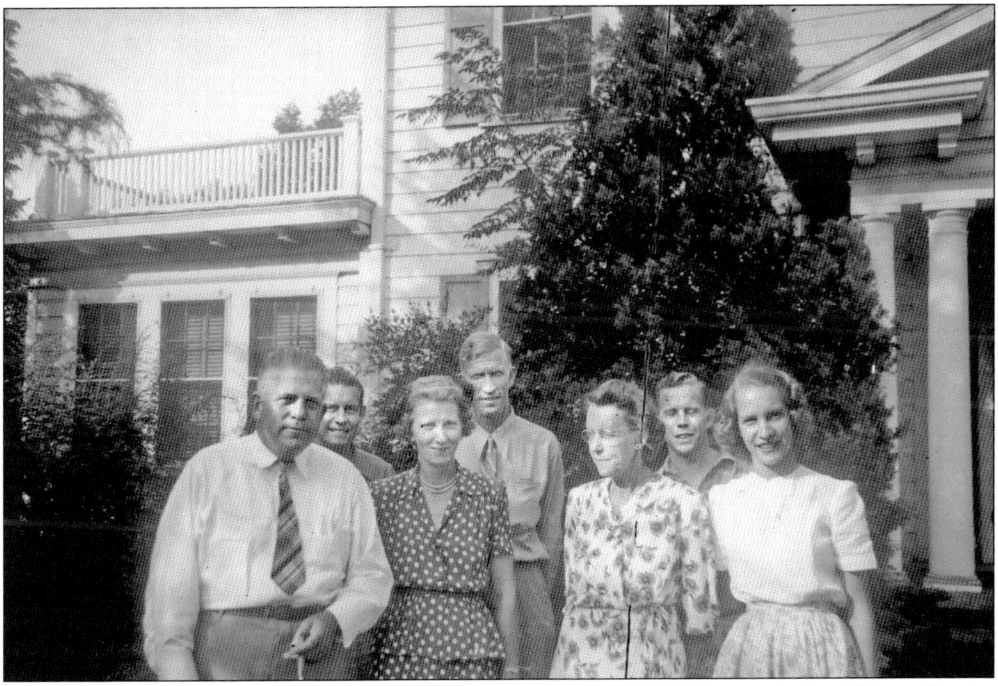

Bobby Gordon took many photographs of his family. From left to right are Arthur Ware, Charles Gordon (Bobby's brother), Sarah Gordon Ware, Marvin Gordon (Sarah's brother), Mary Osborne Gordon (Bobby's mother), Hugh Norris Gordon (Bobby's brother), and Mary Ann Gordon (Bobby's sister). Sarah and Marvin were half-brother and half-sister of Hugh Bingham Gordon, Bobby's father, who passed away in 1932. This photograph was taken in front of their duplex home.

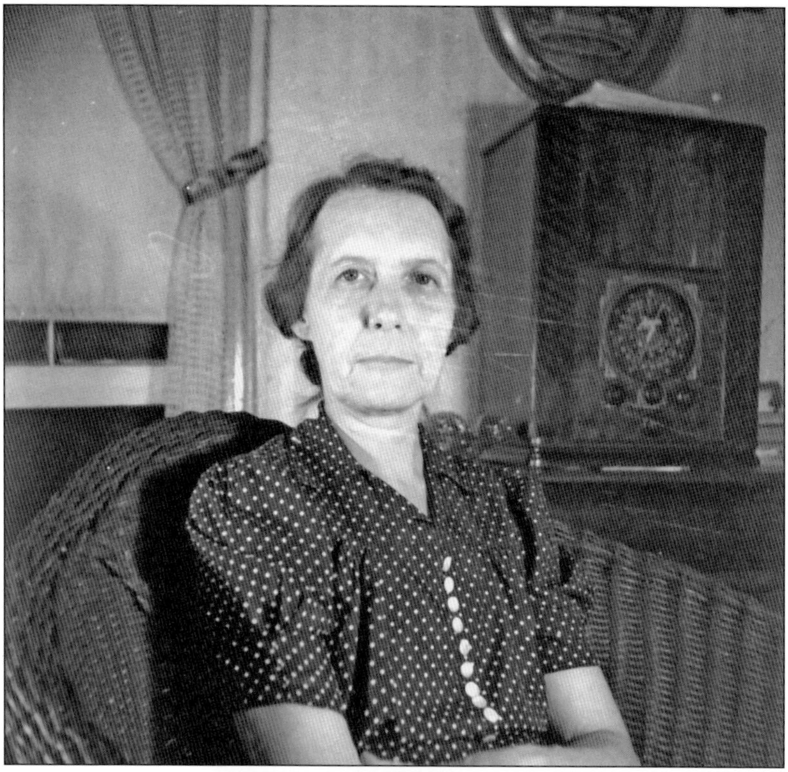

This photograph of Mary Osborne Gordon was probably taken inside her home. She grew up on Flat Rock Road.

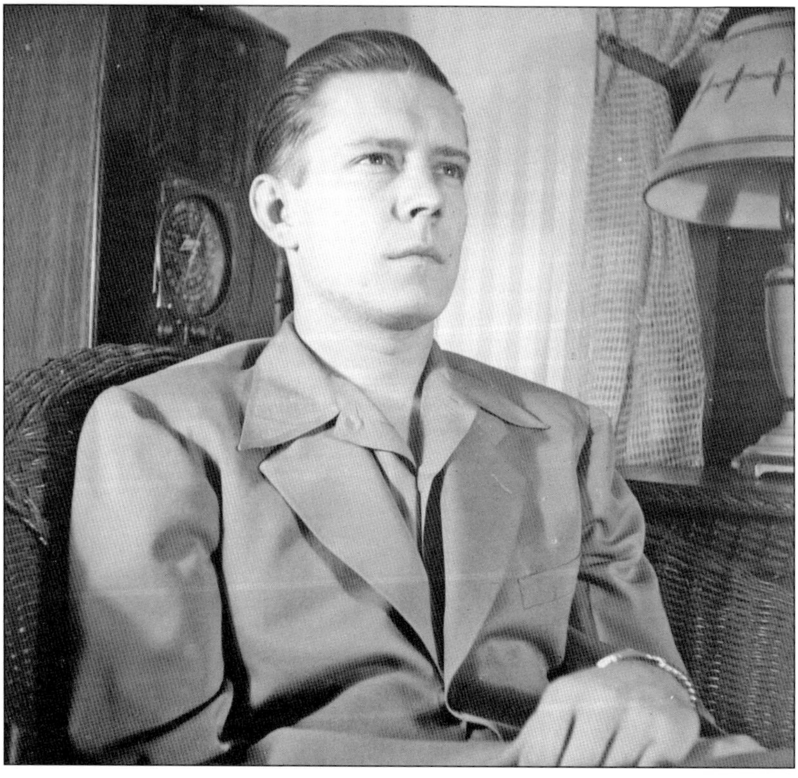

Charles Gordon was Bobby's older brother and the father of Hugh Gordon, who digitized the photographs in this collection.

Charles was a bartender by trade and was assistant manager of the Variety Club of Atlanta for several years.

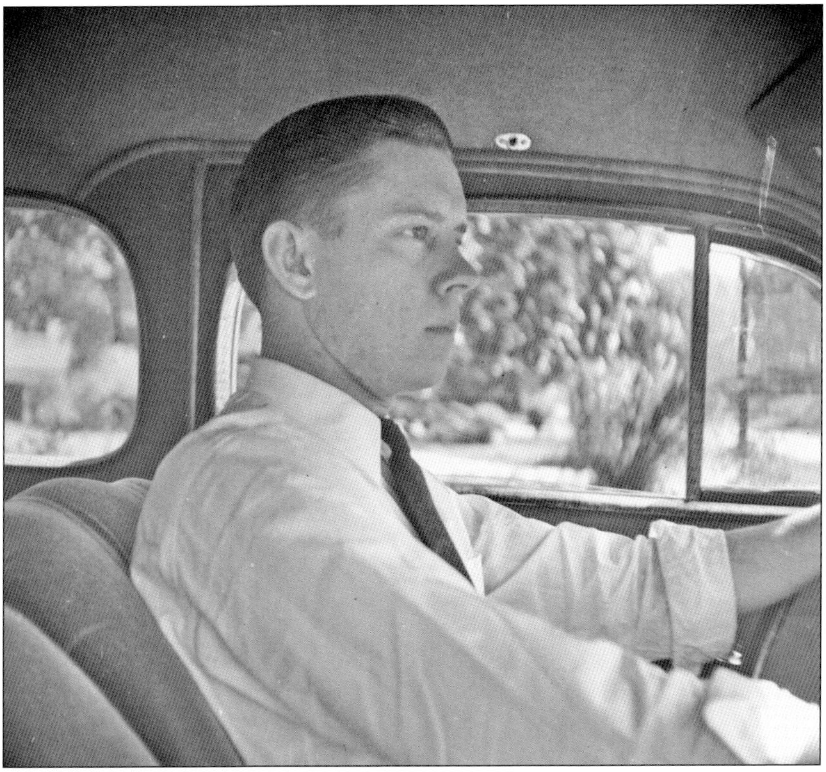

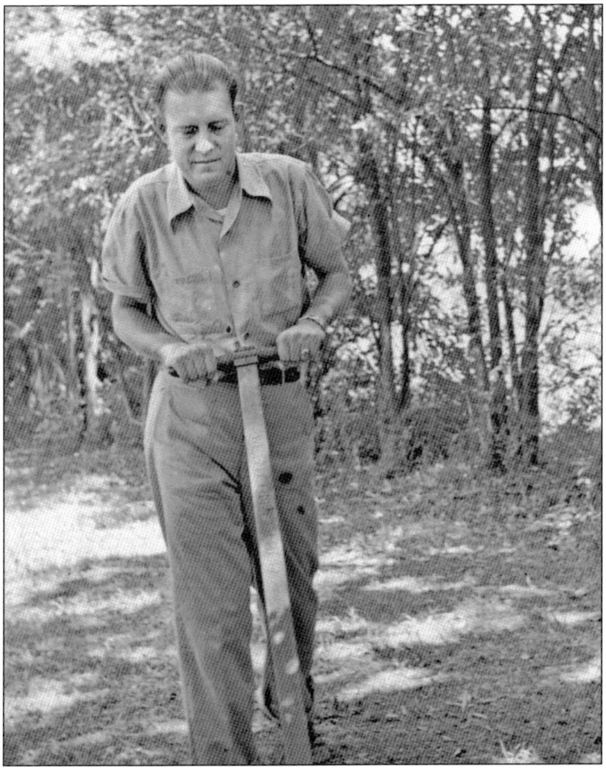

Charles Gordon played basketball in high school. He was a member of the boys' team that played the first game in the newly built gym on December 15, 1933. Other members of the team were William Breedlove, Rhul Dawson, Hollin Breedlove, Marion Nicholson, Shannon Thomas, Ralph Wells, Cordell Berrong, Harry Phillips, Teddy Lundy, and W.R. Weaver. Their coach was Milton Brogdon. They beat Athens High 25-22.

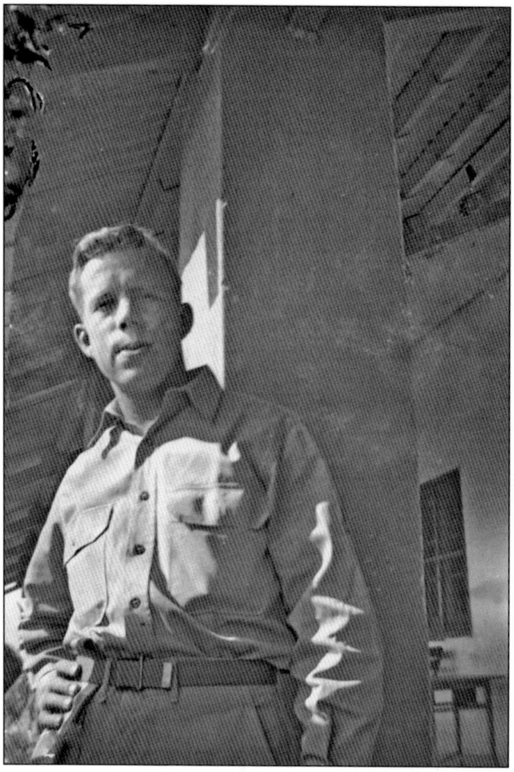

Norris Gordon eventually went to work in Atlanta and married a Methodist preacher's daughter. His full name was Hugh Norris Gordon, and his nickname was "Hambone." Below is a photograph of Norris Gordon dressed in his best suit.

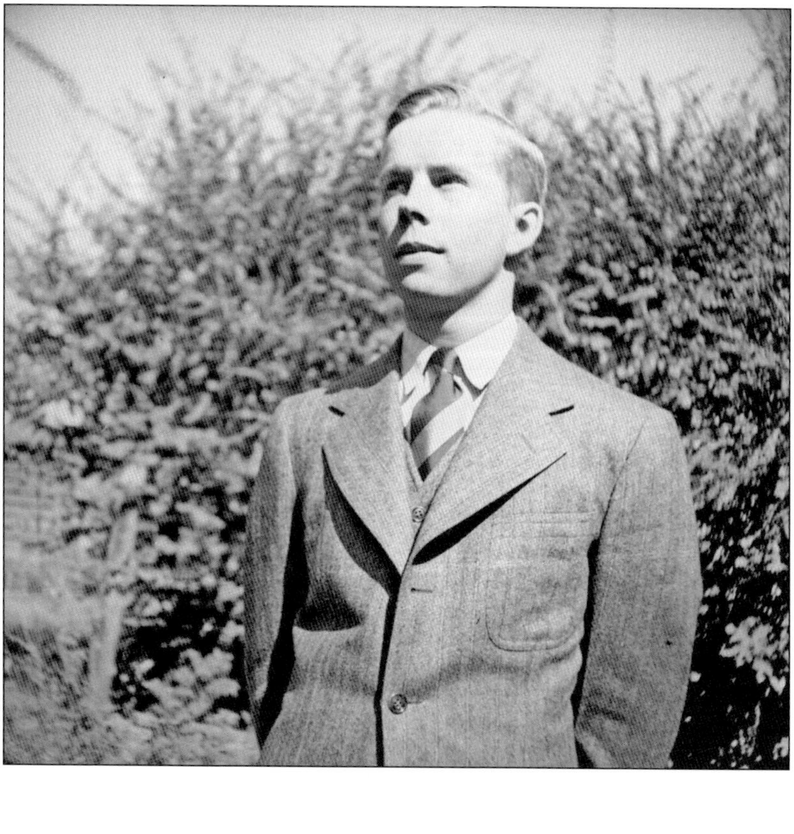

The swing Mary Ann Gordon is using was in the yard next to the Watkinsville Christian Church, which is in the corner of this photograph. The Methodist church across the street is in the middle of the photograph. Mary Ann married Andrew Martin. They had two children and lived in Brevard, North Carolina.

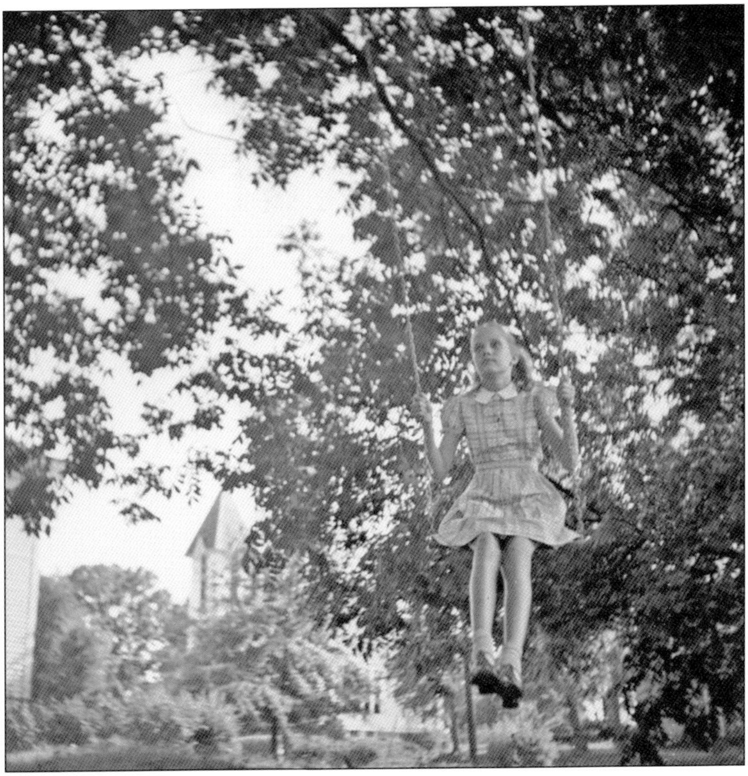

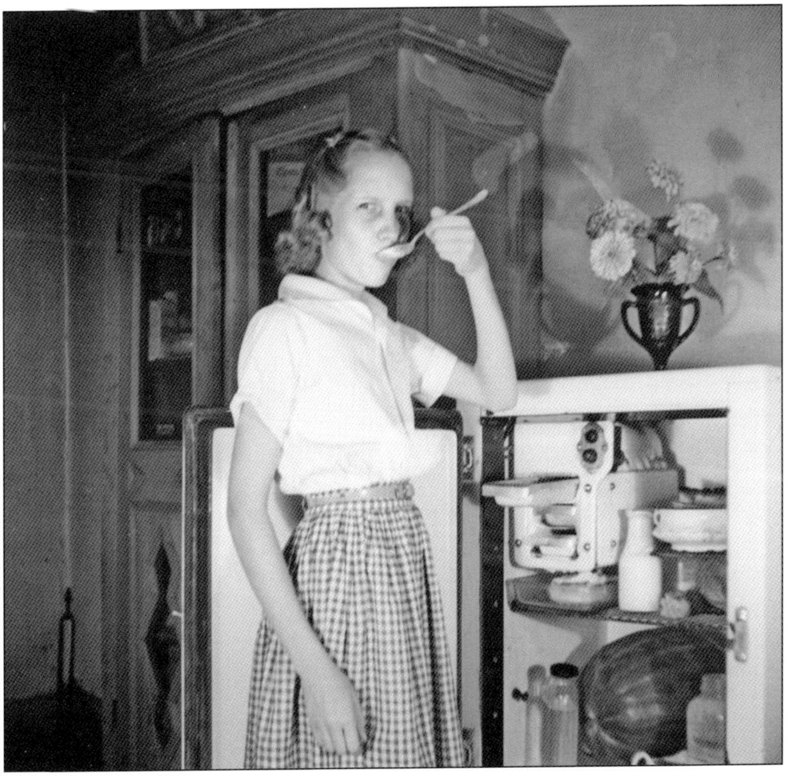

Mary Ann is getting some ice cubes out of the refrigerator. Notice the bottle of milk and the large watermelon.

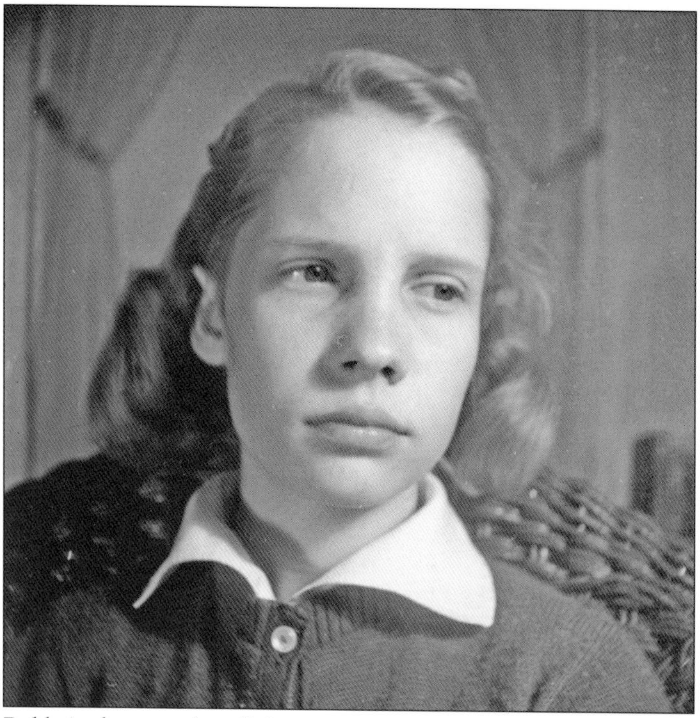

Bobby's photographs of Mary Ann show her growing up from a pre-teen to a young lady. She is a bit older and very serious in the photograph above. She graduated from the University of Georgia and earned a master's degree in social work from Tulane University. She worked in child welfare until she married Andy Martin in 1956. Mary Ann is standing in front of the fig tree in the backyard of the duplex at right. She passed away on May 12, 2018, at the age of 92.

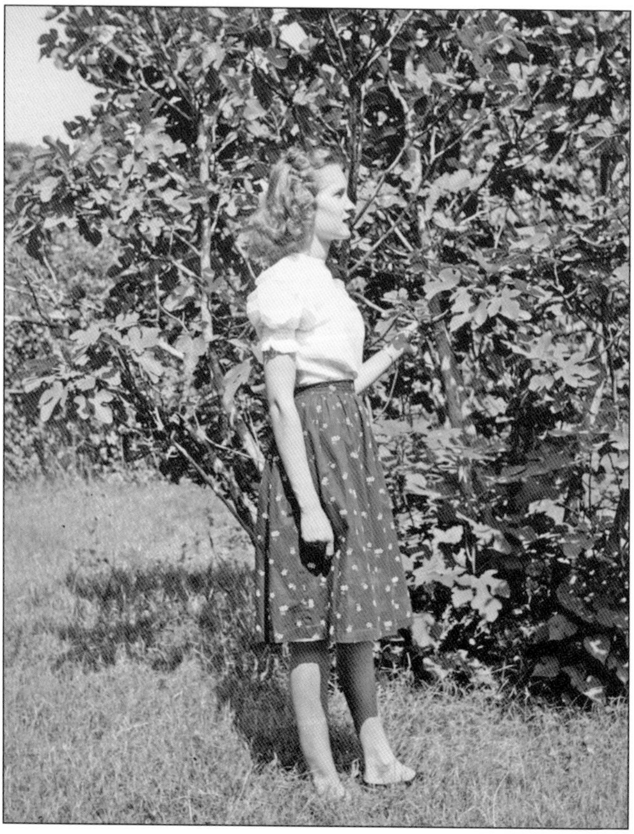

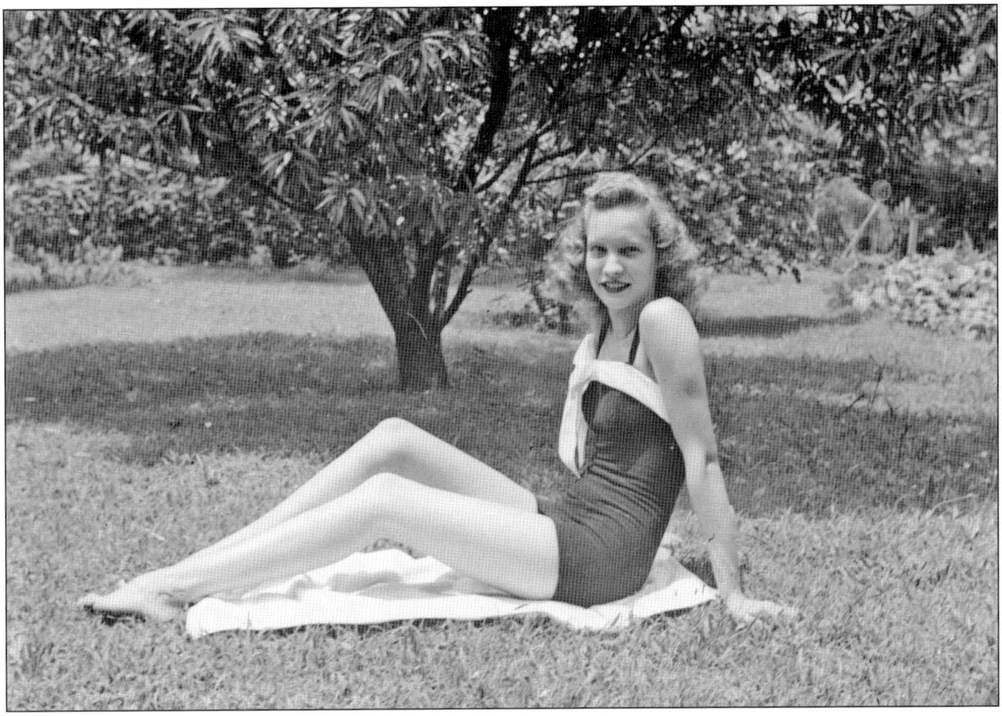

Bobby took several photographs of Mary Ann in this session. Mary Ann and Andy were married 62 years. They moved to Brevard in 1957 for Andy's job with DuPont. Mary Ann had two children and several grandchildren and great-grandchildren. She was one of the founding members of the Brevard Church of Christ, and according to her obituary, she was known for her delicious pecan pies.

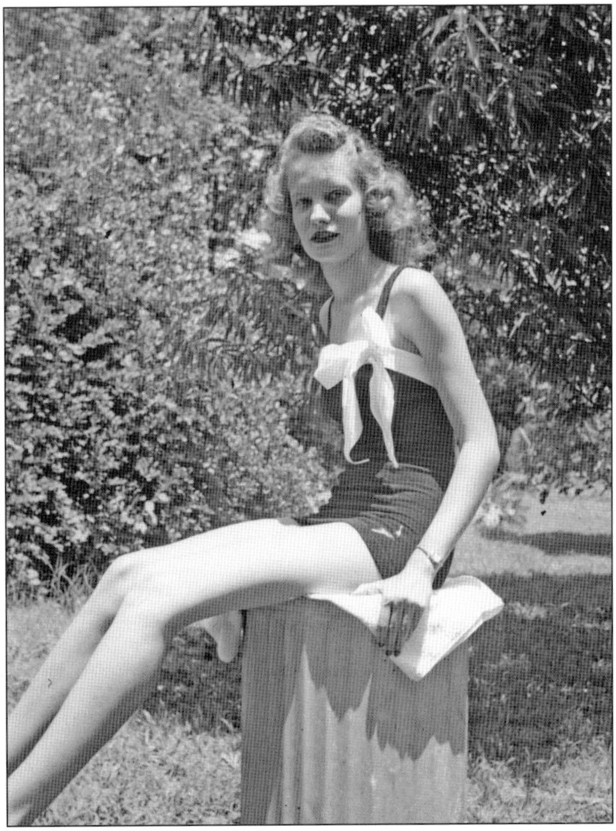

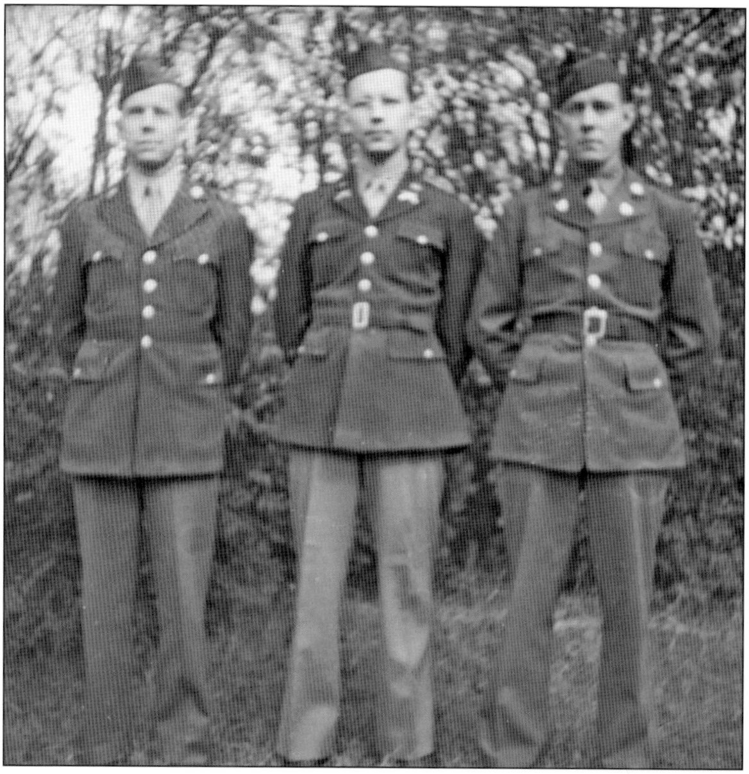

At left, all three Gordon boys (from left to right, Norris, Bobby, and Charles) participated in World War II. Bobby served in the Army as a radio operator with the 106th Cavalry. Charles was a paratrooper with the 17th Airborne Division in Europe, and Norris was a loading supervisor flying supplies "over the hump" (over the Himalayas) to China and Burma. He was stationed in India. Below, Mary Ann took Bobby's place between Norris and Charles for this photograph.

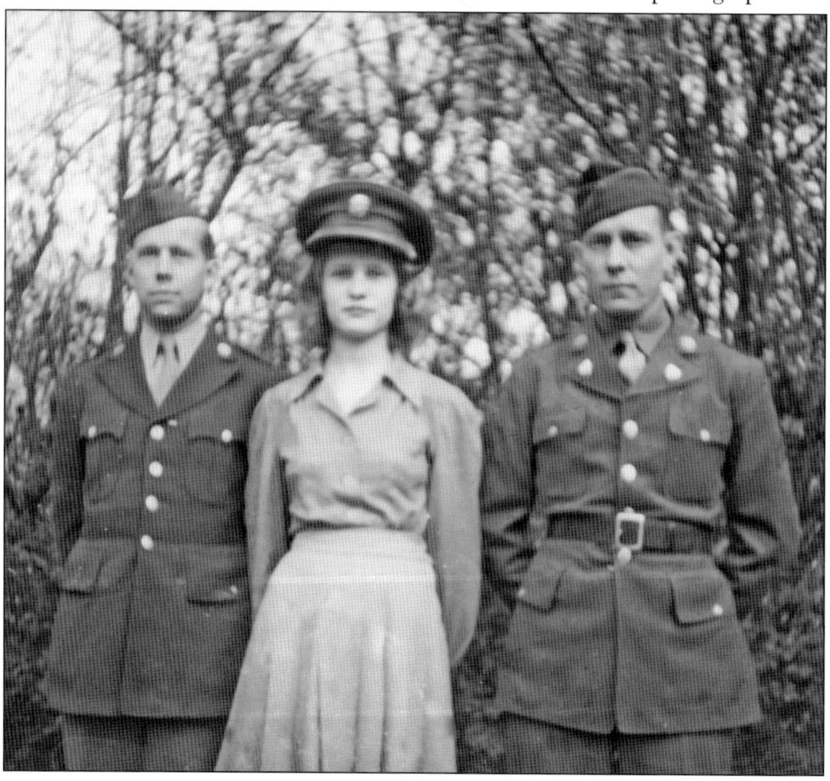

Eight

Winter, Fires, Wrecks, and Fun

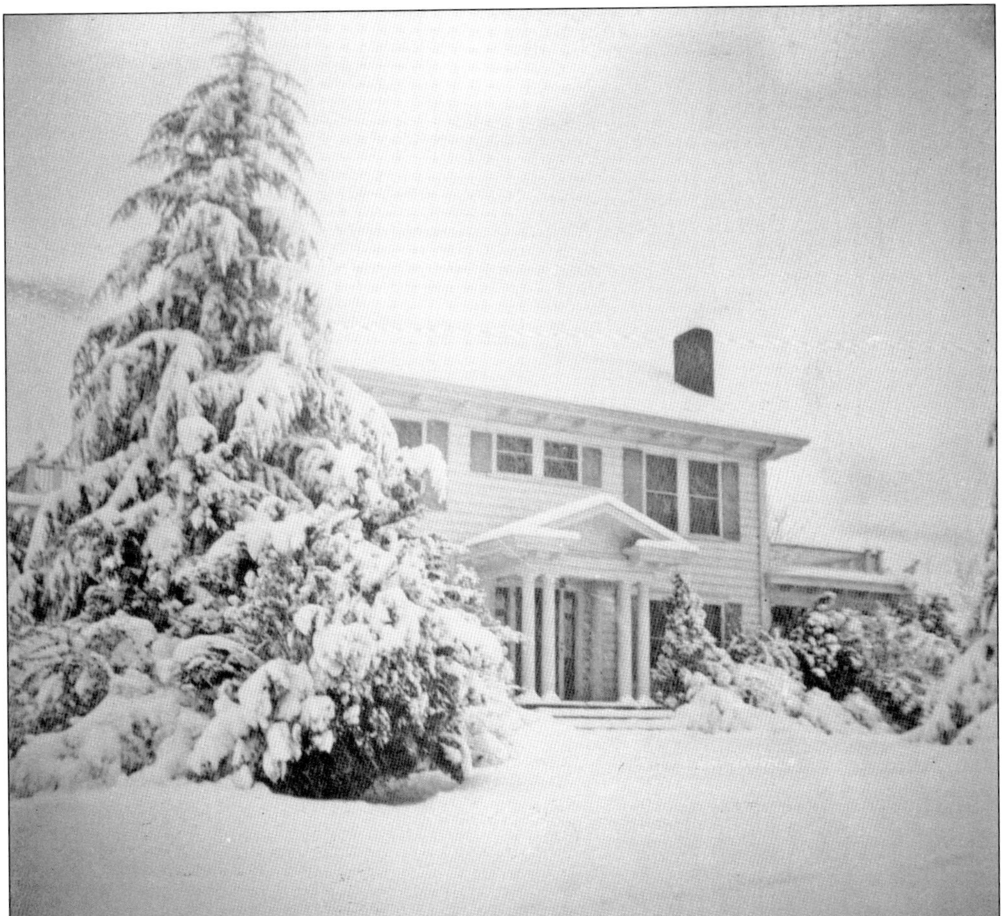

On January 23, 1940, the region was hit by a record-breaking snowstorm. Athens received 9.8 inches, and nearby Atlanta got 8.3. As of 2017, neither of these records has been broken. Bobby grabbed his camera and went outside. This photograph is of his home.

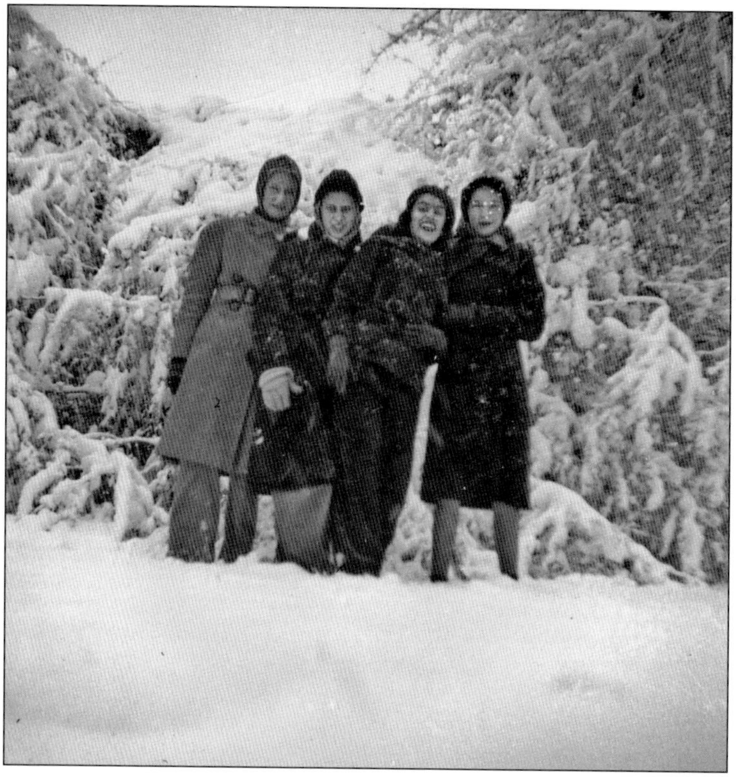

The girls in Bobby's neighborhood joined in the fun in the snow. At left, from left to right, Anita Chandler, Joan Camp, Mary Ashford, and Ann Billups strike a serious pose. In the less serious photograph below, Mary and Ann have switched places.

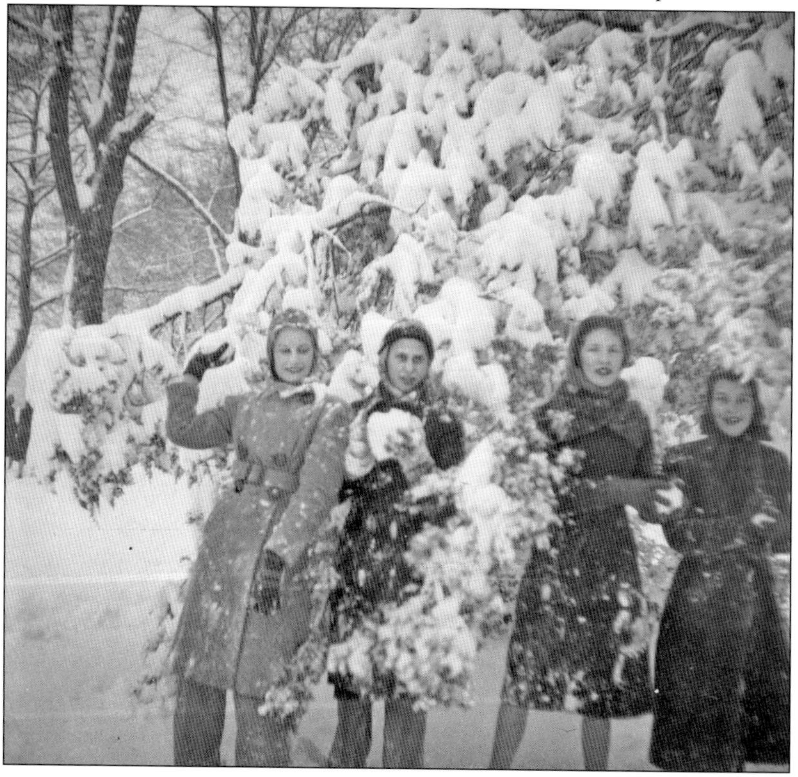

Bobby and his friends made a "snowgirl," which Bobby is posing with in this photograph.

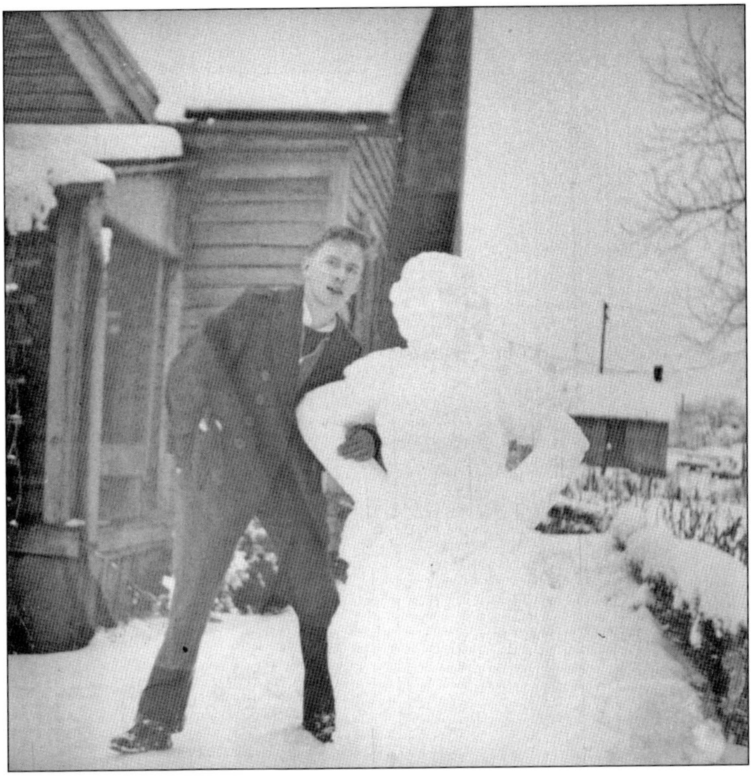

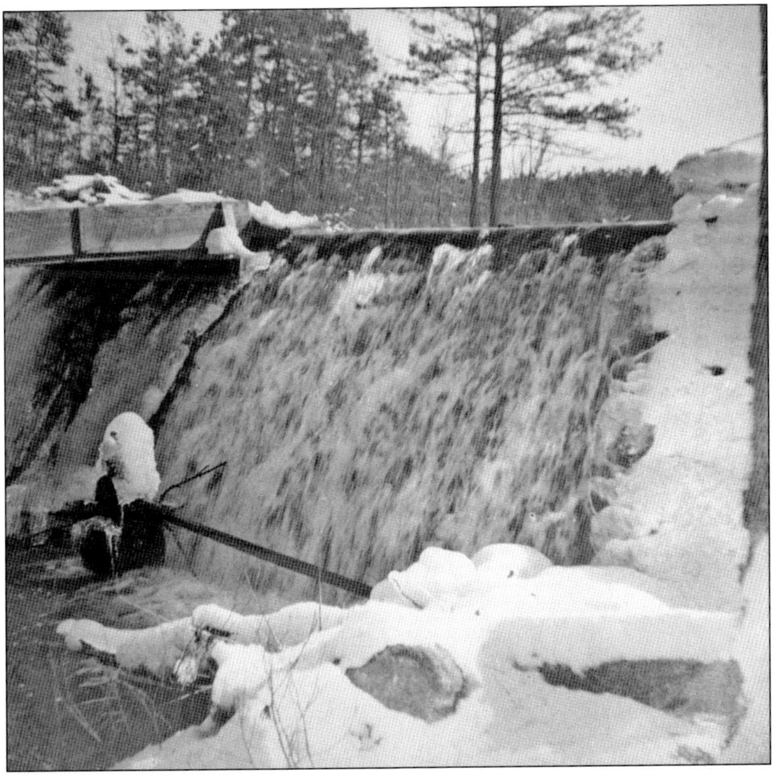

In 1938, the town of Watkinsville voted to establish a water system. This dam is farther up Calls Creek from Harris Shoals. At the base of the falls is the pump and pipe that brought the water to a processing plant downstream.

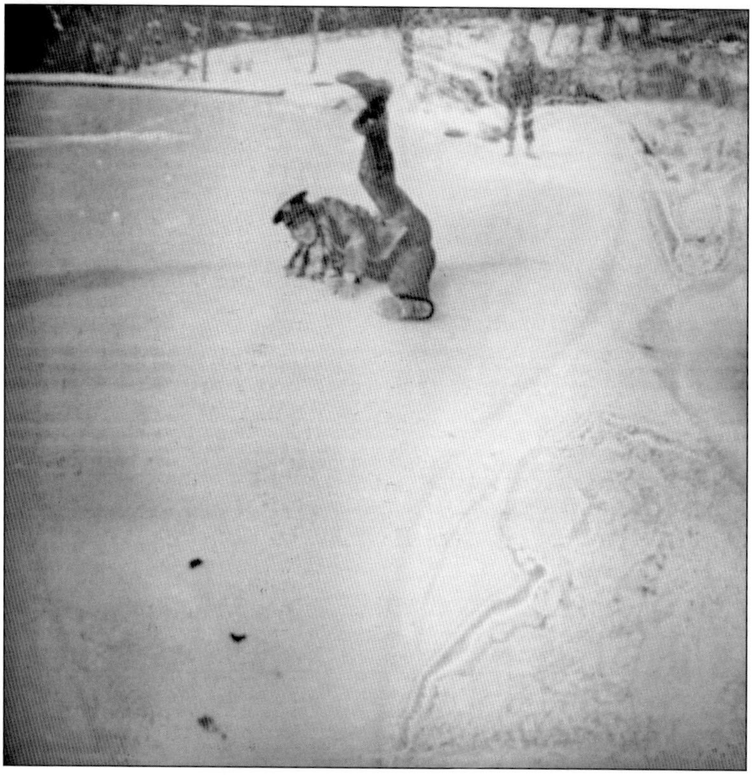

This appears to be the pond behind the dam. The two people playing on the ice are unidentified.

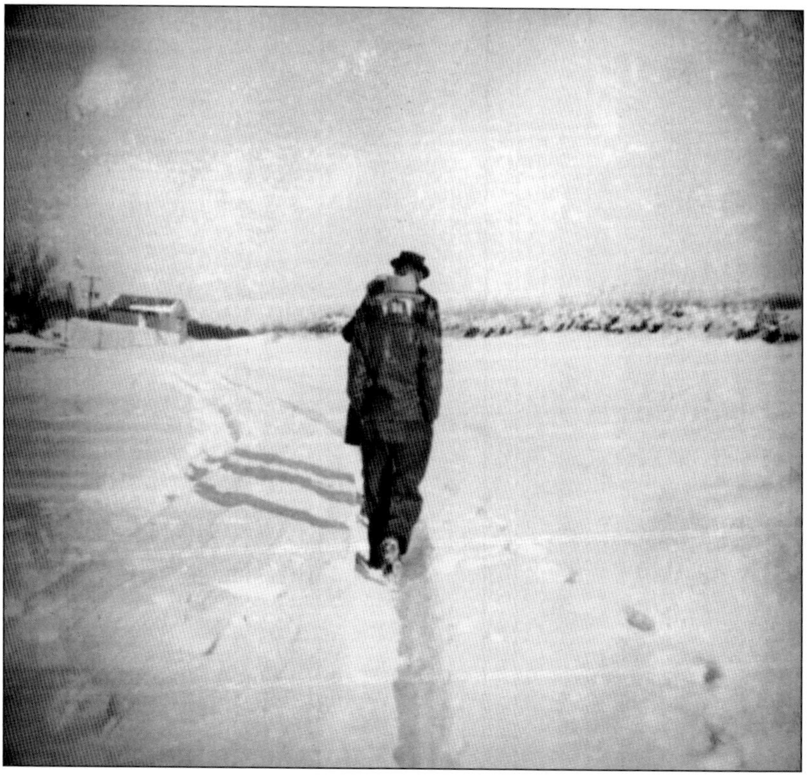

One can get an idea of how deep the snow was from the tire tracks these men are walking in.

This photograph of a cabin outside of town shows how deep the snow was during the winter storm in 1940.

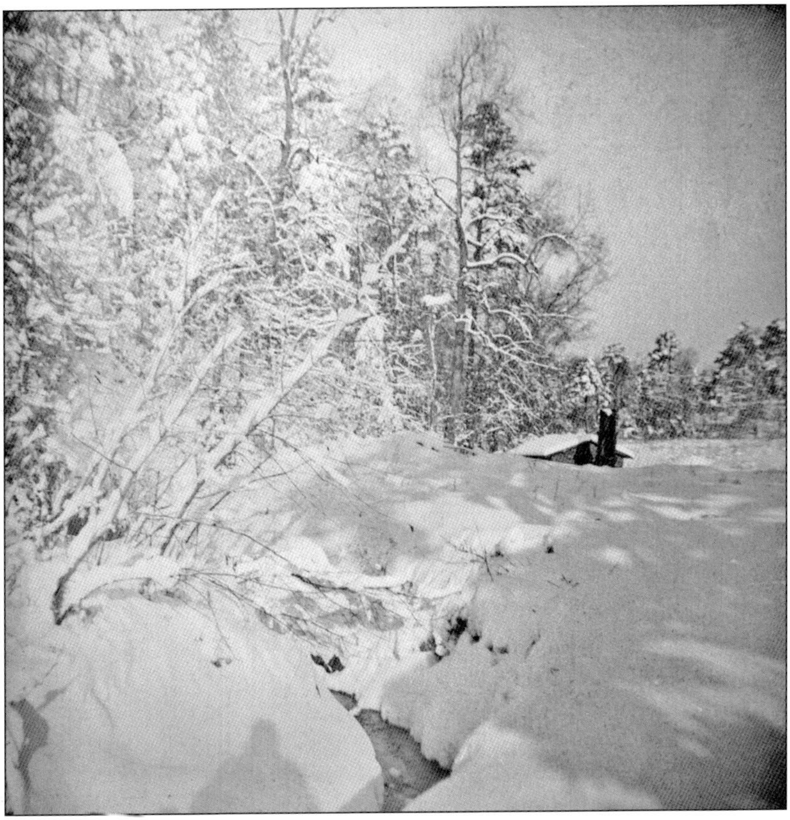

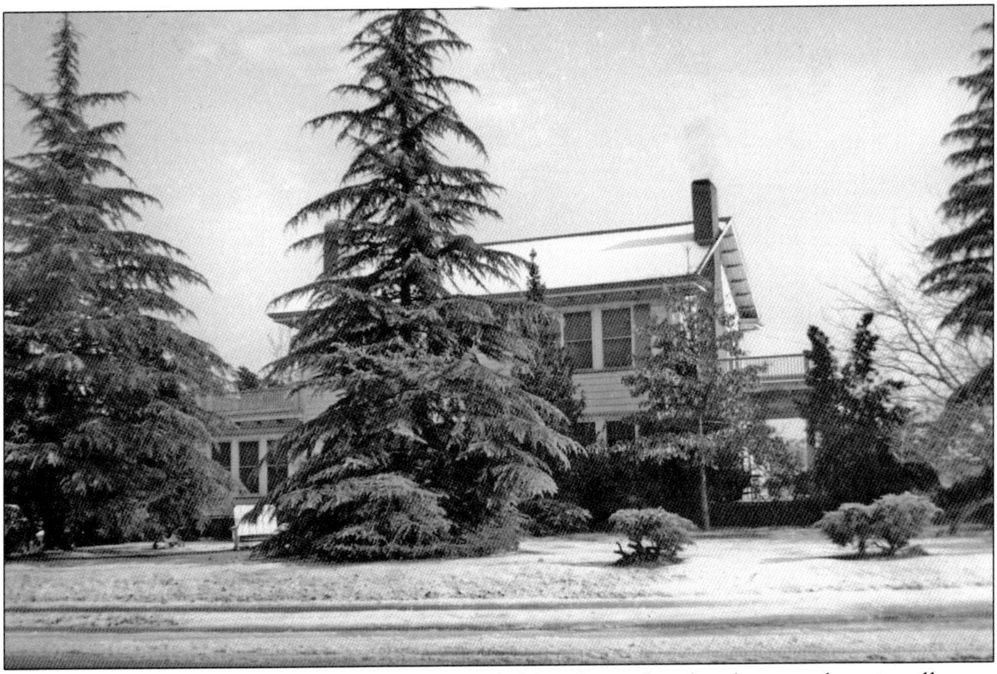

This photograph of the Gordon duplex was probably taken a few days later, as there is still snow on the roof and lawn but not on the trees.

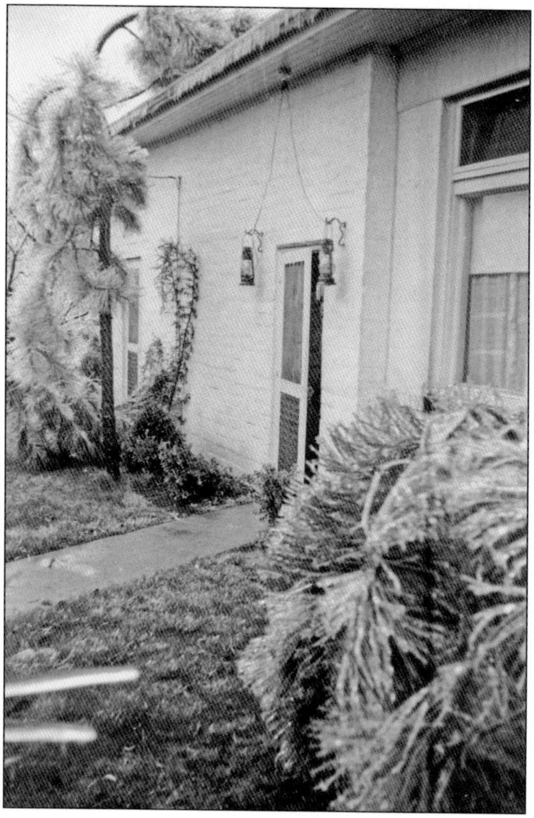

It is more common for Watkinsville to have an ice storm like this one. Notice how the ice is bending the tree by this unidentified home.

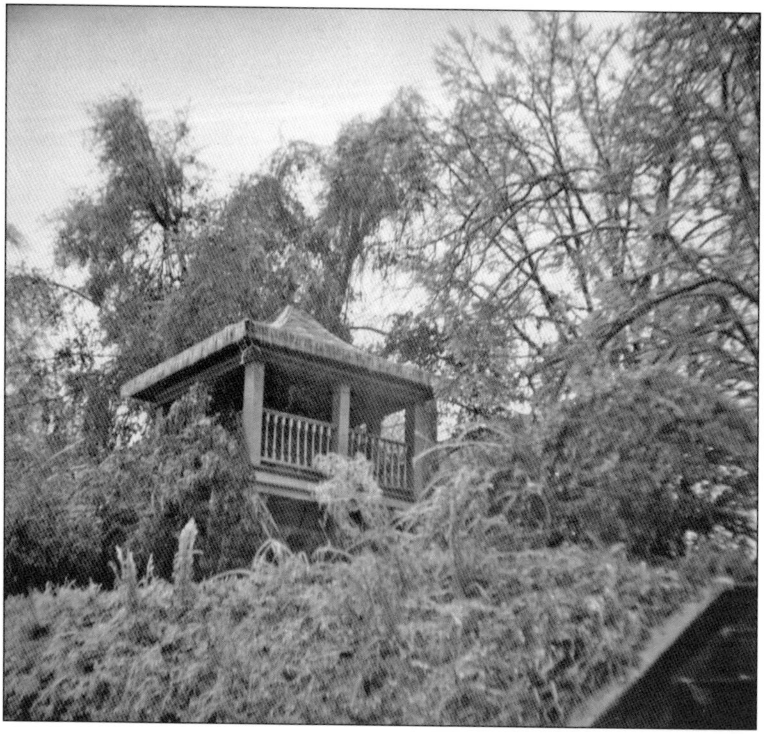

This is the well house that stood on the corner of the Ashford property. The wall at lower right is alongside the steps leading up to the Watkinsville Methodist Church next door.

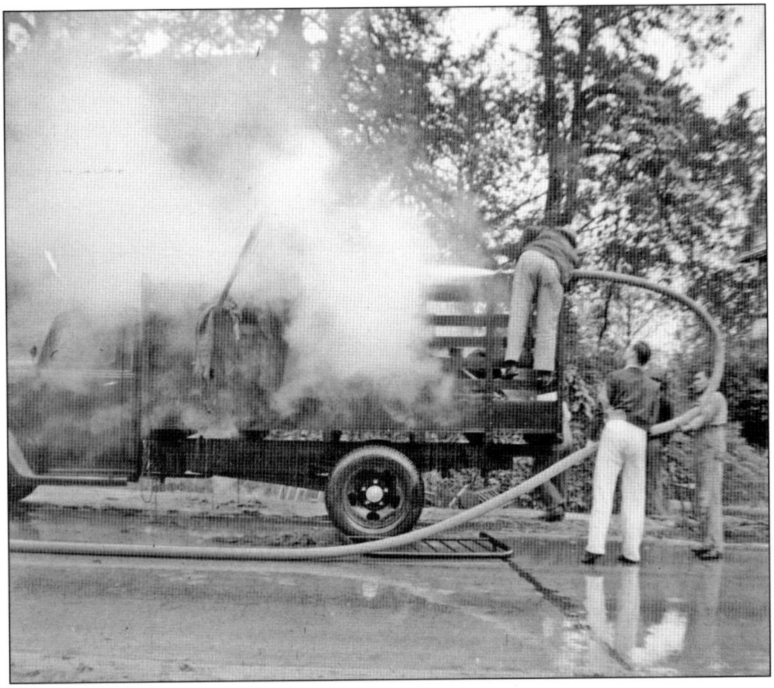

Bobby took these photographs of the town's volunteer firemen working to put out a truck fire.

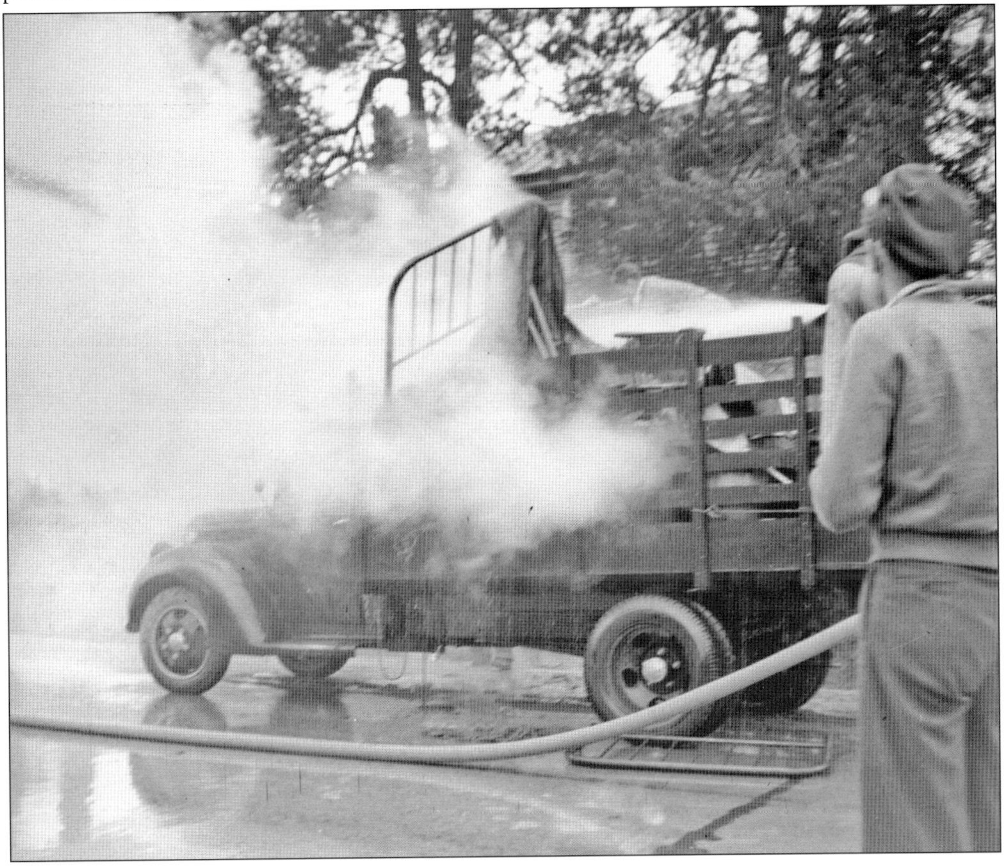

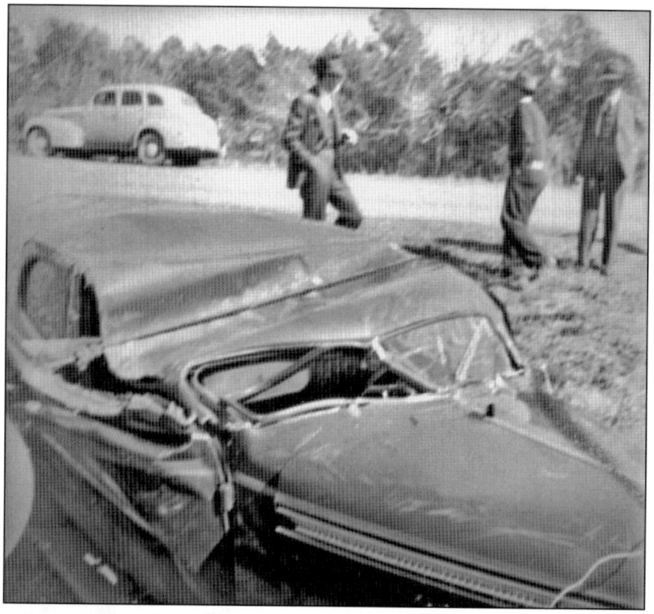

Bobby also took a series of photographs of the men in town investigating a serious wreck. By the smiles on the men's faces, one suspects that the photograph below was posed for Bobby's camera.

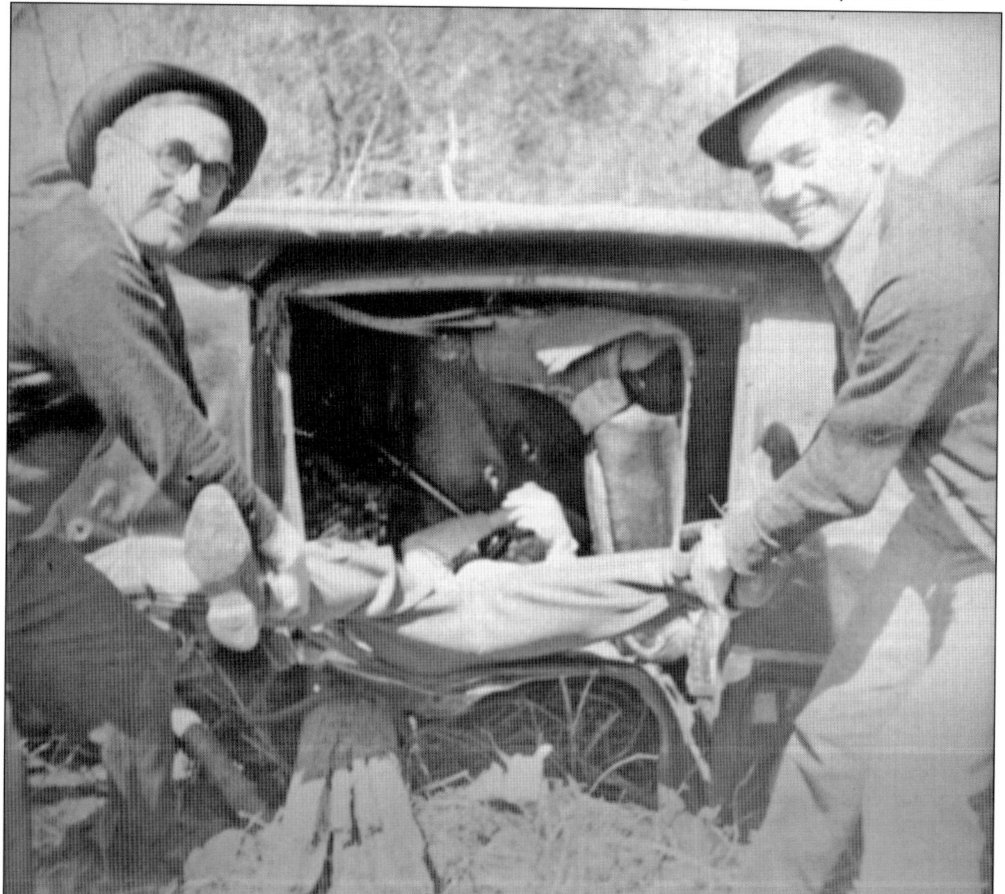

Bobby posed his brother Norris Gordon (right) and his friend Billy Hodges (below) with numbers on their chests. Although Oconne High School did not produce yearbooks during the Depression and World War II years, these may have been taken as senior pictures. Both were members of the class of 1937. Billy Hodges was a pilot before World War II. During and after the war, he taught others how to fly.

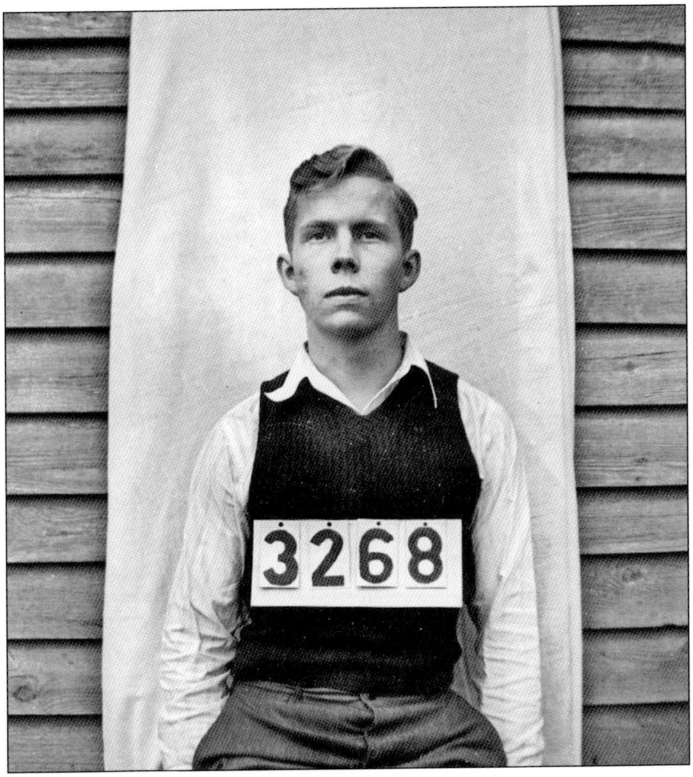

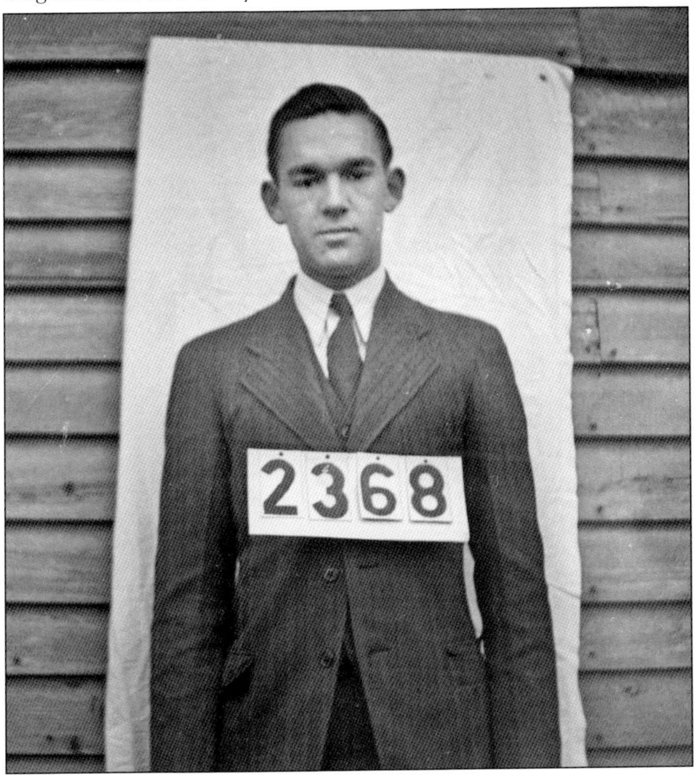